True Course

The Definitive Guide for CPA Practice Insurance

Joseph E. Brunsman & Daniel W. Hudson
Chesapeake Professional Liability Brokers, Inc.

THIS BOOK WAS DESIGNED FOR GENERAL INSURANCE GUIDANCE AND CONSIDERATIONS ONLY.

Dedications

This book is dedicated to all my brothers from the Navy and the Naval Academy who are still Livin' the Dream. Civilian life is amazing, but it will never match the comradery and good times we had together. To my lovely wife, Elizabeth; thanks for putting up with ten months of eighteen-hour days. Even as a civilian wife, you had to withstand another deployment. Without your understanding, this book would still be an outline in my notebook. To my loyal dog Zeus; I could not think of a better companion to keep me motivated at three in the morning. ~**J.E.B.**

To my wonderful family; thank you, for all of your support throughout the years. This book is dedicated to my U.S. Naval Academy shipmates, to those who have served and those that continue to serve. ~**D.W.H.**

A portion of the proceeds from the sale of this book will go to military related charities.

About the authors

Daniel W. Hudson. A United States Naval Academy graduate with an MBA from University of N. Florida, Dan has specialized in insurance for CPA firms for more than 25 years. He holds Chartered Property Casualty Underwriter (CPCU) and Associate in Risk Management (ARM) designations.

Dan served as a Naval Flight Officer, flying more than 550 missions in the Navy submarine hunter, P-3C Orion. He conducted worldwide anti-submarine, littoral warfare and counter-narcotics operations. He served as the Commanding Officer of Patrol Squadron Six-Four (VP-64), earning the prestigious Battle "E." As his final tour of duty, he served as Deputy Commander of Reserve Patrol Wing, retiring as a Captain.

Joseph E. Brunsman. Joe most recently served as a Lieutenant in the United States Navy, working as an Anti-Terrorism/Force Protection Officer responsible for over a billion dollars' worth of equipment and 280 military personnel. Prior to that, he served tours as a Combat Information Center Officer and an Electronic Warfare Officer. During his enlisted time he was an Information Systems Technician specializing in HP-Unix database management, network security, and satellite communications.

Joseph is a 2003 graduate of New Mexico Military Institute and a 2010 graduate of the U.S. Naval Academy in Annapolis, MD, where he obtained a degree in Systems Engineering with a focus on robotics system interoperability. He enjoys powerlifting, business theory, and all things technology related.

Words from the authors

Forty years ago, very few people knew the invoice price of a new car; even the salesman. If the price was anywhere, it was locked in a vault, and only the sales manager had access. This led to an imbalance of power firmly skewed towards the seller, with the buyer hoping not to be taken advantage of.

Under any circumstance where one party has superior information that is unavailable to the other, an adversarial environment will arise. If you look at most of the most popular books for sales professionals, they are rife with allusions of "Always be closing," "Never leave without a sale," and, much to the chagrin of the two former military officers previously deployed in support of real-life operations, "Every sale is a war." These pressure tactics have always been morally questionable, but now, more so than ever before, they're becoming obsolete; and rightfully so.

Now, when you go to buy a vehicle, both buyer and seller have near equal access to information. Buyers can come armed with historical repair costs, internet reviews, crash-test ratings, and, of course, the invoice price; sometimes for multiple vehicles. Today, the world is edging ever closer to having both parties in a transaction with near parity of information. For instance, a doctor will soon be able to analyze mountains of information coming from a tracker on your wrist, enabling hyper-personalized health recommendations. Car insurance companies can now track your vehicle in real time and provide lower premiums based upon safer driving practices.

Information parity will ultimately lead to buyers being more satisfied with the sales process and the product. When sellers clearly define what their product is and is not, they deal with fewer dissatisfied customers. Furthermore, they can tailor their products over time to better serve their customers. As a whole, the sales process becomes less about one party overcoming the other and more about both buyer and seller defining problems and reaching solutions.

Unfortunately, the world of insurance for CPAs is still working on the same model as the car salesman from 40 years ago. The nearly 30 years of knowledge distilled in this book is our attempt to change that dynamic on a national level. As with the previous examples, we firmly believe that this can significantly benefit both our profession and yours.

This book is not only for the benefit of CPA firms across the nation. We spent countless hours writing the book we wish we had as a guide when we began our journey in this profession. As you progress further through this book, you will notice that we focus only on professional lines specific to your profession; namely, professional liability, employment practices liability, cyber, registered investment advisory, directors and officers insurance, and excess insurance. As a firm, we consciously choose to hyper-focus our daily efforts in these areas. We would rather be experts in a few areas than marginal in many.

Noticeably absent are health insurance, business owner's policies, commercial general liability, etc. Simply put, we don't have any expertise in these fields, so we feel that they are better left to others. We have attempted to make this book as up to date and relevant as possible. However, insurance is primarily regulated by the states, and there are untold numbers of different insurers per state. It would be impossible for us to explain every nuance of every policy in every state.

We urge you to use this book as a *reference*. It should never be a substitute for a broker or legal professional who is knowledgeable with your practice and the particular requirements of your state.

You will also notice that there is no chapter on how to get the cheapest insurance. As with any market, there will always be a race to the bottom, but we have found that this can lead to serious compromises of service and coverage when you need it the most. The cheapest insurance is no insurance at all.

In the back of the book you will find our contact information. Over the years we will be updating and expanding this book based upon inputs from CPA firms across the nation. If you have any questions or comments, we would appreciate your input on how to make this book better serve your needs.

Regards,

Joseph E. Brunsman & Daniel W. Hudson

"Journalism is printing what someone else does not want printed; everything else is public relations"

—George Orwell

Contents

Professional Liability Insurance

Professional Liability Loss Prevention

Employment Practices Liability Insurance

Cyber Insurance

Registered Investment Advisor Insurance

Excess Insurance

Directors and Officers Insurance

Additional Information

Professional Liability Insurance

Chapter 1

Professional Liability Insurance Basics

"People always ask me, 'Were you funny as a child?' Well, no, I was an accountant."

—Ellen DeGeneres

Professional liability insurance is the bedrock of safety for a CPA firm. As our area of expertise, and the single most prevalent form of professional insurance for our CPA clients, it is covered extensively in the coming chapters. In full disclosure, we are unaware of <u>any</u> requirement from the AICPA, the PCAOB, or the SEC for you to carry professional liability insurance. Some states will require you to purchase insurance, but that requirement typically only applies to firms with a net worth less than $1 million.[1] However, certain business structures may require insurance, or will afford additional protections.

Professional liability insurance for CPAs covers damages resulting from the allegation of a negligent act, error or omission resulting from providing professional services. Notice that we said, "allegation." Even with flawless accounting during your career and impeccable internal controls, it is still possible, and likely, that a claim will be brought against you.

In our experience, roughly two-thirds of claims are made regardless of flawless accounting work. Even a sole proprietor doing tax returns and bookkeeping needs insurance. Sadly, we tell you that from our experience. Every single CPA in the nation should carry professional liability insurance.

We both have technical backgrounds, and often think of Newton's third law when reading through policy language. "For every action, there is an equal and opposite reaction." When applied to insurance policies, this means that for every increase in policy length, there is an equal and opposite decrease in the comprehension and interest by most CPAs reading it. Unfortunately, this has allowed for unknowledgeable or, in some instances, opportunistic brokers placing inappropriate insurance.

Our goal is not to make you an insurance professional. It is our mission to give every CPA a basis of understanding for their insurance policies and to offer loss prevention strategies, hopefully rendering their policy unnecessary. While this won't necessarily make us any new friends in our profession, it will enable you to come to your renewal from an educated position. This should ultimately allow you to make better business decisions, lower instances of claims and potential claims, and sleep better at night.

Before you begin, it should be noted that these chapters are not based on finding the cheapest insurance policy. As a professional in a field that has daily claim pressure, you will almost always save more money in the long run by working with experts from the start. As always, if you are ever in doubt, consult a trusted broker or legal professional who is familiar with your profession.

Chapter 2

Warning Signs

"Dr. Hoenikker used to say that any scientist who couldn't explain to an eight-year-old what he was doing was a charlatan."
—Dr. Asa Breed – Kurt Vonnegut, *Cat's Cradle*

All of the below are based on our experience of over 25 years specializing in accountants' professional liability. We have not only heard other brokers tell these stories to our clients, we have had inexperienced insurers try to sell *us* on these so-called benefits so that we'd be tempted to represent *them*. We politely refuse, and we recommend you consider the same.

This chapter, more than any other, may bring some discontent our way. Of course, a questionable broker will do everything to convince you that the points below are misconstrued. He might bolster these claims by referencing other prominent firms he has insured. Understand it's a questionable position that should require significant clarification, not anecdotal stories.

Sign #1: "More insurance is better insurance."

Reality: Over-insuring your company is just as dangerous as not carrying enough insurance.[1] If you do end up in court, your own insurer may actually disclose your policy limits.[2] When the claimant determines you have excessive limits on your policy, you may be in for an expensive

3

ride. Additionally, if your insurance company doesn't settle inside your limits, you may have an action against *them* to recover your loss. Your insurance company and defense counsel are obligated to act in good faith to resolve your claim within your policy limits.[3] Only some of the largest CPA firms or those with high exposure may actually need high limits of liability.

Sign #2: "Buy a high separate defense limit to avoid liability limit erosion by defense expenses."

Reality: Most professional liability suits are settled well before trial.[4] Across all areas of practice, the average cost of defense for matters that resolve well before trial is less than $50,000. This cost does not include the cost of expert testimony or consulting. Should your claim not be resolved early or before trial, with continued discovery, depositions and conferences, your defense expenses could reach well over $100,000.

With separate defense limits being relatively inexpensive compared to limits of liability, consider playing it safe by assuming the minimum average cost of defense is $250,000. This cost, or greater, could be your defense expense exposure in a claim that is fully litigated. If you're a very large CPA firm or have a high level of exposure, you might consider $500,000 or greater in separate defense limits. This consideration also holds true if your firm has a higher probability of more than one claim in a year. At a certain point, having your policy limits erode may encourage a faster settlement.[5] Having too much in the war chest may encourage the plaintiff to continue the lawsuit – and prolong the stress for your firm.

Many brokers will argue excessively high defense limits as a selling point, but this argument has little basis in reality.

4

Sign #3: "We've got this new insurer who is an automotive/marine/aviation insurance industry titan. They're new in the market and offering a great policy at a high discount."

Reality: You're likely dealing with a broker trying to sell you a piece of paper that likely has no real expertise behind it. This is so prevalent in the industry that we discuss it in multiple places in this book. We never recommend you pick an insurer with less than five years of experience in the accountants' professional liability. Over the last 30 years, the average lifespan of an accountants' insurer is roughly four years.[6] You don't want to deal with them when they've exited the market. They never gained the requisite knowledge and experience in the first place. Once they're gone, they'll have even less motivation to help you.

Sign #4: "Don't go with any insurer that picks your defense counsel for you. You want to have the decision in your hands; it's your business at stake."

Reality: Imagine if every client came into your office demanding you use a certain page out of the tax code that they found online. You've spent decades honing your craft, and a quick internet search will not make anyone an expert. Insurers with considerable experience have not only seen your specific problem before, but they also know specific lawyers in specific law firms that can deal with your specific situation. For example, we've seen an experienced insurer know that one lawyer in New York City is the best at pre-trial motions for dismissal, but then switch to a defense council out of New Jersey if a claim goes to court. They know that the second lawyer is much better at arguing cases in front of juries. *That* is the expertise that you want on your side.

5

Experienced insurers typically have long-standing relationships with these law firms, who have been trained on your exact policy specifics. Also, insurers usually have arrangements with these firms for lower hourly rates, saving you money with built-in discounts.[7] The NYSSCPA has estimated that this can save you upwards of 30% on defense costs.[8] Ultimately, having your experienced insurer pick the defense counsel isn't for their benefit; it's for yours.

Sign #5: "We've got the same insurance policy the other guy has, but it's 30%, 40%, 50% cheaper."

Reality: Either the broker doesn't specialize in this field or is fully aware of the risk, but advises in favor of the product regardless. Either way, be skeptical. Online tax services and your firm both do personal tax returns, but you can't compare the two. If there were a way to significantly lower prices and still provide the same level of service, the industry stalwarts would have already done so.

We would agree that you'll save money on the front end. However, when an issue arises, you're going to be stuck leaving a voicemail and hoping someone gets back to you in time. In the end, it will always cost you more, be it in money, frustration, or sleepless nights. Shopping for value, not price, is always the best long-term decision. You get what you pay for, especially in complex lines of insurance.

Sign #6: "Insurer #1 will force you to take a settlement, but Insurer #2 doesn't unless you agree to it." (The Hammer Clause Argument)

Reality: Generally speaking, a hammer clause is how insurance companies limit their losses. When a settlement is arrived at with the opposing party, you'll need to agree with that settlement. Modified hammer clauses will allow you to continue litigation with various additional expenses to your firm, such as paying for all additional defense costs and settlements.[9] Remember, the majority of professional liability claims are settled long before they ever reach a court room.[10] Further, the NYSSCPA referred to this type of provision as, "illusory." Very few firms ever object to an offered settlement.[11]

Honestly, you shouldn't *want* to go to court, but sometimes it's just the last available option for your insurer. It's typically cheaper for them to settle out of court than to go the full mile, pay your defense expenses, and potentially have your name put in the paper. Furthermore, trying to explain legal code to jurors from other professions is a dangerous game and almost impossible. After more than two decades in the industry, we have never seen a CPA want to *stay* in court. Almost always preferred is the desire to resolve the matter efficiently and get back to business. Not only is being in court incredibly stressful, but it detracts from your duties at the firm and can evaporate your billable hours. Why continue that?

We spoke with the CEO of one of the largest CPA insurers in the nation. Even with more than 30 years insuring CPAs, he has never once had any firm *want* to stay in court.[12]

Sign #7: "We can get you an unlimited Extended Reporting Period."

Reality: Extended Reporting Periods (ERPs) are covered in detail in Chapter 12. The basic idea is that when you decide to sell, merge or close your business, you have the option to purchase an ERP. This is commonly known as a tail policy. This provides coverage for future claims that arise from professional services rendered from your policy's retroactive date to the date you purchase the tail policy.[13] In our experience, the only insurers who will offer you an unlimited ERP are those who are new to the market and have no expertise with your profession. Keeping potential claim reserves on their books *forever* is fiscal suicide. They're promising to keep a cash reserve on hand until the end of time on the off chance that you get sued 20 or more years after you shut the lights off.

Ideally, this is a really great option for your business; you'll be covered eternally. In actuality, you're dealing with an insurer that does not understand the ramifications of their actions. In our experience, they will most likely not survive the next few years in the accountants' market. In the unlikely event that you have a suit arise in 10 years, you'll be dealing with people who probably haven't defended a CPA's claim since they left the market.

Have you ever wondered why you aren't required to keep all of your work papers and forms indefinitely? It's because the probability of needing them 20 years from now is incredibly remote.

The main players in the industry generally don't offer unlimited ERPs, but they do offer the periods that a claim would be likely. It's one of the reasons they're still around.

Always keep in mind: a true professional won't fabricate a crisis for your firm. They will provide you an honest, plain-language assessment and offer solutions to any problems that you may have.

Chapter 3

Four Simple Questions

"Simplicity is the ultimate in sophistication."

—Steve Jobs

During our service as naval officers, we each became intimately familiar with the concept of operational risk management. Planning for an operation and having contingencies for a multitude of scenarios assured safe and effective employment of our weapons systems and increased the probability of mission success. In the heat of a complex mission, when resources were challenged and critical decisions needed to be made, we focused on efficiently assimilating information and directing attention to the core risk. While this method may seem simple, it has proven time and time again to enable effective decision-making, reasoned sorting, and maximization of resources in a stressful environment.

In today's marketplace, your firm could literally have dozens of *seemingly* equal professional liability policies from which to choose.[1] On top of that, you have very specific considerations when it comes to insurance. Is your firm expanding, contracting, or holding steady? Are you planning on merging, acquiring, or being acquired? What is your scope of practice? Are you considering expanding the services offered? Do all your partners even agree?

When you come to a consensus regarding your firm's profile, you will need to understand the policy language. Then, begin an educated debate on limit adequacy, exclusions, coverage agreements, and so forth. Each decision could have unseen future ramifications for both your reputation and the survival of your firm. Selecting a policy requires significant due diligence on your part.

We can tell you firsthand that when we review a new client's previous policy, many are simply chosen on price and a brief representation. The professional liability policy you choose can cost tens of thousands or even hundreds of thousands of dollars. Such an expensive and important part of your firm's future should not be left to chance.

Below is a set of heuristics: four questions you can ask to help determine which insurer is right for your firm. While deceptively simple, they can save you time and money. They can also save you the heartache of partnering with the wrong broker and insurance company. One of the most important lessons we learned as naval officers was that everyone has answers, especially salesmen, but only a few will ever ask the right questions.

1. How long has this insurer been offering this product?

Liability insurance itself is a very broad category. It is only loosely associated across different fields of the profession. A company that does not specialize in this highly complex line will have difficulty correctly handling your subpoenas and most potential claim scenarios. Experience in handling these matters is critical for the long-term survival and prosperity of your firm.

If they've been in the marketplace for *less than* five years, you're talking to the wrong insurer. According to Ric Rosario, President and

CEO of CAMICO, "There is a claims lag, the time difference between when work was performed and when a claim was resolved, whenever a new insurer enters the marketplace. This lag could last anywhere from 3–8 years, depending on the severity of claims and scope of practice for covered firms. When new insurance carriers charge a premium, they often don't know if their premiums are right until the seventh or eighth year. It is all too easy in the early years to have no data and to undercharge a premium only to get burned later down the road. This happens quite often in long tail insurance such as professional liability."[2]

When a new insurer inevitably takes losses, the knee-jerk reaction is to raise their rates. Then every opportunistic salesman gets the word and comes knocking on your door. When a CPA firm inevitably sees their rate inexplicably increase, they jump ship and join another insurer for a cheaper premium. The result? Yet another company is out of the marketplace, and you're back where you started.

If you're one of the unlucky few who is dealing with a claim and have an insurer who has left the marketplace, don't expect a pleasant experience. They are bound by the policy terms and conditions, but you can imagine how responsive they'll be to your needs. Longevity with an insurance carrier is key, especially if you are interested in stability and excellent service for your practice.

2. Are your matters handled in-house, or outsourced?

Insurance companies with less experience will often outsource many services. There is little telling whether these firms have any experience dealing with CPA matters. The cheaper your insurance and the newer the insurance company, the more likely it is that your firm is going to have an inexperienced and overburdened service provider handling your matter. To attract, train, and retain the caliber of professional you *want* to solve your problems takes decades and a very specific company culture. These seasoned professionals, like all people, value job security. Being industry insiders, they realize that taking a job at a new account- ants' insurer is not a stable long-term decision. In full disclosure, this type of experience is going to cost you extra on your premium.

Compare this extra expense to the billable hours lost as your part- ner waits in frustration for his 1-800 voicemail to be returned. Protecting your firm is not something you want to take chances with. You really do get what you pay for.

At your next renewal, ask your broker who, by name, will handle your problems when they arise. If they give you that 1-800 number, you may have a problem.

3. Does the carrier offer *real* risk management services?

Loss prevention is one of the most valuable services offered to a firm. Many carriers will state that they offer "Risk Management or Loss Pre- vention Services." Many times these services are not offered by a specialist, or else it is just another 1-800 number and outright window dressing. Be sure your firm is receiving the best possible advice. Loss prevention protocols can help prevent or minimize claims and keep your premium in control for years to come.

When you are considering an insurer, be sure to ask about the pro- fessionals providing these services. Inquire about their credentials and availability to assist you quickly with any issues. Preferred carriers offer a CPA or CPA/JD specialist to address your questions. This could range from helping you with engagement letters, responding to a sub-poena, or how to properly disengage from a client. Experienced risk management services can prevent unnecessary claims and future head-aches for your firm.

4. What limits do they offer, and why?

This may seem counterintuitive, but experienced companies won't nec-essarily offer you the highest limits. Once again, this all comes down to market experience. The actual rates and availabilities for account-ants' professional liability insurance are based on a host of factors. These include annual revenues, risk exposures based on scope of prac-tice, loss experience, quality control, and the work history of the owners/partners. This type of forecasting takes years of experience and an intimate knowledge of the CPA profession.

Furthermore, different lines of insurance follow boom-and-bust cycles, which are nearly impossible to predict and are separate from the economy as a whole. When entering the market, a new insurer doesn't know if the market is on the upswing or headed down.[3] Experience in other liability markets simply has little bearing.

Any new insurer offering excessively high limits at a bargain price, should be a serious red flag. If you're worried or unsure about your limits, consider working with a specialized broker. They should be able to speak intelligently about your specific exposure, loss prevention, limit adequacy, and coverage. Most brokers are more than happy to sell a high-limit policy, but few have dealt with or understand the claims process specific to CPAs. Excessively high limits of insurance will of-ten just put a bigger bullseye on your company, potentially lengthen the claims process, and can hasten an inexperienced insurer out of the market.

———————————————

These four simple questions will not only provide specific answers, but should give you a good feel for both the broker and the insurer. Moreover, a knowledgeable broker should be able to answer these questions easily and without hesitation. If you aren't receiving prompt and knowledgeable answers, it's time to reconsider that relationship. As a professional, you shouldn't be taking chances on amateurs.

Chapter 4

Professional Liability Policy Specifics

"The most valuable commodity I know of is information."
—Gordon Gekko

B y now, you should have narrowed down the possible choices
of reputable insurers and brokers. The next step is to compare the specifics of policy and program. Remember, it would
be unrealistic to assume that any insurer will cover every possible claim.
Ultimately, it's up to you to determine your requirements, but there is
more to consider than just the cost of a policy.

Due to the inherent complexity of policy language, if you're ever
in doubt, work with a trusted broker and consult a legal professional.
They can help you decipher the policy.

Now, let's get familiar with the minimum insurer and policy specifics that you should inquire about:

Who is the issuing company, and who is the program administrator?

Contrary to popular belief, there can be a difference between who is
offering you a policy and who is paying the claim. Managing General
Agencies (MGAs) will often be the program administrator, meaning
the "face" of the program and the people you will generally interact

15

with.[1] The MGA administrates the program. They provide marketing, underwriting, policy issuance and claims assistance to the issuing insurer.

The issuing company is the actual insurer standing behind the policy. As we will cover later, we don't recommend you do business with a program administrator who has a history of constantly changing issuing companies. You don't want the final decision-makers being new to the market, because chances are they won't be there for long.[2] Issues can arise if the insurer handling your claim has left the market and no longer has a relationship with your MGA. An exited insurer may not be as motivated to handle your claim with their "best foot forward."

Does the insurer offer free CPE courses?

Depending on the size of your firm, this can save you thousands of dollars every year. The most sophisticated insurers will offer specialized CPE that covers a complete range of topics. Furthermore, they may offer live webcasts, in-house seminars, and everyone's favorite, self-study courses.[3]

Does the insurer offer a free online reference library?

This is an often underutilized resource that can save time for even the most senior accountant. Superior online reference libraries will contain information on A&A, including SSARS-21, subpoenas and depositions, fraud prevention, identification theft, tax issues, and engagement/disengagement letters.[4]

Does the insurer offer subpoena services, and how much do they cost?

Some policies may offer unlimited services free of charge,[5] other policies will have a sublimit, be subject to your primary limit, or be completely silent within your policy. Experienced insurers should have in-house subject matter experts with significant subpoena experience. Some insurers have a long-standing relationship with outside legal counsel, but advice may be subject to your deductible, limits of liability, or a cap on subpoena expenses.

What is the policy territory?

Depending on the insurer, policy territory comes in a few different flavors. Some have worldwide coverage regardless of where the claim is brought, others offer coverage only in the U.S. and its territories, or Canada. Typically, suits tend to be brought before U.S. courts due to our mature legal system. Check your engagement letters for the agreed-upon venue. Be sure to consider applicable laws, and your firm's specific requirements.

Now that you have narrowed down the insurers that may meet your program requirements, let's look at the minimum policy specifics you should consider:

Does your insurer offer defined premium credits?

Insurers may offer an orientation program to familiarize you with their services, and encourage early reporting on claims and potential claims (as defined later in this book).[6] Others may offer credits dependent upon a clean claims record or certain loss prevention measures.[7] We recommend you work with a company that will monetarily incentivize your firm to take full advantage of their resources and early reporting.

Does the policy offer deductible reductions?

Look for policies that offer deductible credit for early reporting of potential claims and the use of alternative dispute resolution (ADR). This can lead to a 50% deductible credit generally ranging from $25,000 to $50,000. The credit can vary widely, dependent on specific wording. Regardless, early notification of a potential claim is typically required to meet policy requirements.[8]

Also, question how the use of ADR measures may affect your coverage. Certain insurers will offer a deductible credit only when a claim is <u>resolved</u>, while others will offer credits for <u>seeking</u> a resolution. In terms of protecting your balance sheet, consider a policy which offers protection by <u>seeking</u> resolution. Also ask how the use of ADR will impact your coverage if no resolution is reached and you want to proceed with litigation.

If you do end up in court, or other proceeding, will the policy pay your loss of earnings?

Coverage in this area can differ substantially. Check to see whether there is a per-day, per-claim, and aggregate limit for your attendance in mediation, arbitration, or trial proceedings. Some policies are completely silent or offer no provision. Other insurers may offer this as an endorsement but may charge an additional premium.

Does your policy pay for regulatory or disciplinary proceeding expenses?

Depending on your specific scope of practice or the type of clients you service, you may be subject to regulatory proceedings. Every firm faces the possibility of a disciplinary investigation; commonly the result of an ethics allegation brought by a former client. Most policies will pay legal expenses, but only up to a limit of $5,000 to $50,000. You may also be subject to a per-event limit or a per-policy-period aggregate limit.

Does the policy put a percentage cap on outside interests?

Nearly every policy will limit coverage when there is a financial interest. Many policies will exclude professional services rendered when the aggregate ownership of insureds, including affiliates and related individuals of insureds, is currently or was ever greater than a certain percentage. This percentage usually ranges from 10% to 20%. While this may seem trivial, consider the connectedness of the world. You wouldn't want to be caught without coverage if an employee (considered an insured) happens to have an equity interest in a client.

What is the policy definition of "Professional Services"?

Though often overlooked, this can make or break your firm. The definition of professional services should be as broad as possible. It should be crafted to cover all aspects of your professional services. Be sure to determine whether pro-bono services are covered. If you are engaging in investment advisory services, know the coverage. Insurers shy away from these services due to a disproportionately high propensity towards claims.[9] Also, check to see if there is coverage for the purchase or sale of securities and insurance products. Many insurers will explicitly exclude this from coverage. The possible need to purchase a separate RIA policy is covered later in this book.

Who is considered an "Insured" under your policy?

As business practices change, and the use of temporary and contract staff becomes more prevalent, this clause is becoming more important.[10] A proper policy should cover all your staff, as well as temporary and contract workers. It should also cover predecessor firms and merged or acquired firms if you assumed their prior professional acts. Be sure all of your subsidiary or affiliated businesses are accounted for.

Who is considered an "Innocent Insured?"

Given that most insurance policies exclude coverage for intentional misdeeds, it's imperative that coverage is contemplated for innocent parties. This can come into play if, say, a partner is alleged to have intentionally violated a law by helping a client misstate elements of his tax return. In this instance, the remaining partners who were fully unaware of the circumstance may still qualify for coverage under the innocent insured provisions.[11] Pay attention to the clauses that specifically state what defines an innocent insured and what criteria they must meet to maintain coverage.

Is there mention of "Misappropriation of Client Funds"?

Look at the scope of practice for your business. If you have assets under management or can write checks for clients, you should pay special attention to this wording. Many policies are silent on coverage, and others expressly deny or limit coverage. Some may offer anywhere from $50K to $100K, or full policy limits for misappropriation of client funds by your staff. If this is a major concern for your firm, you may want to consider raising your primary policy sublimit or purchasing a separate crime policy.[12]

What is the policy definition of "Damages"?

This specific clause will help you determine what your insurance company is legally obligated to pay. Certain policies exclude fines and penalties but include tax penalties assessed against a client if you made tax errors. Generally, most insurers exclude punitive damages, though some will include them if required or allowed by law, which can vary by state.[13]

What is the limit of liability, and is it in excess of your deductible?

With a retention, the limit of liability is in excess of your deductible. A deductible is a part of the limit. If you're carrying a high deductible, you may have a significantly lower limit available than you thought. Consider per-claim, split-deductible, and aggregate deductible options.

What are the "defense provisions" in the policy?

In most policies, your insurer has the right and duty to defend you.[14] Some insurers will have the right to appoint counsel, while others are silent on the issue, and still others will let you appoint your own counsel. As mentioned previously, insurers committed to the accountants' market will have subject-matter experts available. This saves both your firm and your insurer time and money, while having the necessary background to adequately defend your firm.[15]

Having the right to appoint your own counsel is generally neither within your range of expertise nor in your best interest. The hourly rates may be much higher, the specialization of your selected counsel may not be present, and your recourse against your insurer for a "blown" defense may be limited.

What are the claim settlement provisions?

In particular, look into the hammer-clause-vs.-no-hammer-clause argument that is mentioned in Chapter 2. In most instances, a hammer clause will never actually be used. The NYSSCPA has called the necessity for this clause, "illusory."[16] Most claims are settled long before trial. Once in a trial situation, most firms just want to get out of court and get back to business.[17]

Others will have a "modified" hammer clause. Here, you will pay a certain percentage over the cost of settlement and legal fees if you decide to disregard the settlement recommendation from your insurer. Of course, this is subject to various other conditions. While the percentage varies depending on the policy, it can range upwards of 50%.

Some insurers will have no hammer clause whatsoever, mentioned either explicitly in their policy or not at all. In this instance, you are likely obliged to accept the settlement reached by your insurer.

Again, by the time a settlement is offered, you will likely be more than ready to get out and back to business.

Does your policy offer an Extended Reporting Period (tail policy), and are there additional provisions?[18]

The ERP is covered in greater detail later in Chapter 12, but we'll go over the basics.

An ERP is typically purchased during a merger, acquisition, dissolution, non-renewal or cancellation situation. The intent of an ERP is to cover claims made in a selected future period arising from professional services rendered. This is from your retroactive date through the termination of your current policy. Your policy will include a provision for this option.[19] The duration of the period in which you can report a claim or potential claim varies by insurer. Some policies offer an option for a free ERP to a CPA's estate if they were a sole proprietor that died or became disabled. Other general options may include an option for qualifying partners to also purchase an ERP. Periods for an ERP can vary from one year to an unlimited term. Due to the importance of an ERP, always seek a professional broker and qualified legal counsel to look over the specific provisions.

Does your policy offer coverage for emotional distress and mental anguish?

Frankly, it sounds like an unlikely requirement, but these allegations may be added in an attempt to increase payouts. Typically, a professional liability policy will exclude coverage when these allegations are brought in conjunction with a claim arising from bodily injury or property damage. This is reasonable, as these claims are covered under a separate policy, usually a business owner's policy (BOP) or commercial general liability policy (CGL). They may cover these claims if they are included in a claim arising from alleged libel, slander, or invasion of privacy. Depending on the insurer, they may or may not include these damages.

Does your policy cover the managing of investments?

In the Registered Investment Advisor Insurance section, we'll go over the possible need to have a separate policy for these types of activities. Depending on the policy, you will have various exclusions or endorsements. Most policies have an exclusion for broker-dealer activities, but may include your registered investment advisor (RIA) activities. Why? Broker-dealers deal with the looser idea of suitability, whereas RIAs have a strict fiduciary duty and are more tightly regulated.[20] Remember, having a policy dedicated to your specific investment activities can provide superior coverage and greater insurer expertise.

Is there coverage in the policy for services rendered to publicly traded clients?

If you currently engage or seriously plan to engage these types of clients, ensure there are no related exclusions. Speak with your underwriter and broker prior to engaging a potential or current SEC registrant. Be very certain that your policy can support this significant exposure. Underwriter scrutiny can also extend to unregistered investment vehicles, as well as Reg A, Reg A+ and Reg D offerings. Due to the nature of their businesses, publicly traded clients are constantly open to litigation, and, by extension, your services will very likely be scrutinized.[21] You wouldn't want to find yourself suddenly without coverage or with a strict coverage limitation for one of your largest clients.

Does your policy offer cyber coverage?

Cyber liability and its associated costs are becoming increasingly important to address. Further in this book there is an entire section devoted to the topic. For the purposes of this chapter, we will explore common wording within a professional liability policy.

Many professional liability policies will cover third-party exposure and defend you at a civil proceeding concerning a violation of Privacy Breach Notice Law[22] or any law referenced under the definition of Privacy Injury and Identity Theft. Ask if credit monitoring, notification expenses, and other first-party exposures are covered. These requirements can add a very large and often overlooked cost if you experience a cyber event. Some policies may offer smaller sublimits or a limited scope endorsement.

Don't be surprised if there is no coverage whatsoever. A good number of insurers are still noticeably silent on cyber liability, as they struggle with how to deal with this relatively new issue.[23]

Read your policy carefully to determine your coverage and whether a separate cyber liability policy is warranted. Unfortunately, the odds are against you, so be prepared.

Is there a sublimit for late reporting a claim?

Because most professional liability policies we've seen are claims made and reported style, you need to report both claims and potential claims within the specified period, or you can be denied coverage. As least one insurer we know of will offer an additional $100K sublimit to assist with claims which are reported late. This is incredibly beneficial for any number of scenarios, and we've seen it come in handy more than once. If available, seriously consider this coverage.

Does your policy offer continuity of coverage?

Of the few industry stalwarts, there is only one insurer we're aware of that offers continuity of coverage. This may sound like a minor detail, but make no mistake, continuity of coverage is a game changer in the industry. With certain provisions, it allows for the late reporting of potential claims. [24] Though that may seem insignificant, late reporting a potential claim is one of the single most prevalent reasons for a denial of coverage. If you want the partner group to sleep better at night, seriously consider seeking out this coverage option.

What other odds and ends are covered in your policy?

Each insurer has its own unique policy language and offers various additional program elements. This can include crisis management coverage, PR consulting, small limits for employment practices defense, coverage for merged or acquired firms, community service D&O, and cyber options.

Though all of this may seem daunting, remember that your professional liability policy is the cornerstone of protecting your firm. When in doubt, ask your broker or appropriate legal counsel. We promise, they'll be happy to discuss it with you.

Chapter 5

Professional Liability Exclusions

"Lawyers spend a great deal of their time shoveling smoke."
—Oliver Wendell Holmes, Jr.

Your policy is a statement of your coverage and benefits, as well your responsibilities. As with other contracts, never assume that your failure to read and fully understand your policy is a likely defense.[1] Under most circumstances, your insurer has no duty to explain your policy or its exclusions.[2] Regardless of the length of time you are claims free or the total premiums you've paid, never expect an insurer to make an exception to your policy.

The below is a list of common exclusions found in accountants' professional liability policies. Every policy is different, and they can vary by state. At a minimum, pay close attention to your coverage agreements, definitions, exclusions, and endorsements. Policies are generally fixed, but an endorsement can be agreed to modify coverage for a specific situation.[3] Talk to your broker about any modifications you may require.

Before we begin, it's helpful to know that an "insured"[4] refers not just to the partners or management of a policyholder's firm. Depending on your policy, this could include a current or former owner, partner, shareholder, or employee of your firm; predecessor firms; and

27

temporary or contract employees for professional services performed on the behalf of your firm. Communicate clearly with your insurer to confirm that your policy covers the individuals and entities you require. Review your policy and ask your insurance broker or legal counsel questions.

Claims made by an insured or related individual against another insured are usually excluded.

Under your policy, *insured* usually means your partners, employees, and, in some instances, contractors. For example, a claim made by an employee's relatives against your firm may not be covered. Also, an insurer may argue that providing professional services to relatives is a conflict of interest and impairs your independence as stated by the AICPA.[5] Additionally, most claims which involve one insured against another, are usually employment practices claims,[6] internal disputes, instances of collusion,[7] or management-decision type claims that may be covered under a D&O or other type of policy.[8]

Claims connected with the services of any insured who acted as an employee, officer, or director of any company, business, or charitable organization not named in your policy may be excluded.

Many of your partners and staff are likely involved with charitable organizations. This is a common method of both supporting your local community and making potential business contacts. Claims that arise out of acting in these capacities are probably not going to be covered. In short, they do not cover all of your outside activities.

Any claim, even if they relate to professional services you render, in which an insured was at any time managing, controlling or operating a separate entity, may be excluded.

This exclusion often impacts CPAs who provide temporary or interim CFO services, or who serve in a fiduciary role such as trustee or executor, or as a director or officer for an outside organization.[9] These situations should be addressed with your insurer to confirm whether coverage is, or could be, offered under your policy.

Any claim from an entity, even if related to professional services you render, in which the insureds under your policy own more than 10% to 20% of that entity, may be excluded.

The percentage depends on the insurer, and, to our knowledge, there is no discernible standard between states. Once again, insurers want to avoid a conflict of interest or collusion by disallowing an insured the ability to sue themselves.[10]

This exclusion can impact a CPA that has engaged in a business venture or invested in a business with a client. CPA insurers must ensure that they are not seen as insuring any outside business against failure.[11]

The part of any claim where a client is seeking reimbursement of fees for professional services rendered are generally excluded.

This exclusion falls under the category of business risk. Claims must be made for damages and are not meant to guarantee the work of a firm. If, for instance, a client complains that your services were inferior and demands their money back, the reimbursement of fees will not be covered.[12] You should, however, still consider reporting the circumstance to your insurer. It is probable that the reason behind the request for fees is a matter that should be reported as a potential claim. This will help preserve your policy rights should the matter later evolve into a claim.

Punitive or exemplary damages, to typically include fines, sanctions, and penalties, unless required by law, are almost always excluded. [13]

In many states, these damages are excluded by the states themselves. The notion of a punitive damage is a method from an authority to create a deterrent to poor behavior. By allowing an insurance company to pay these damages, states believe that the increase in premiums from insurance companies would transfer the burden of increased awards to innocent parties.[14] In many instances, the state board that governs the insurance industry in that state will disclose if an insurance company is allowed or required to pay these damages.[15] Check with your broker and state board to determine what you would be required to pay.

Bodily injury and property damage claims are generally excluded from coverage.

Once again, your insurer is limiting the scope of their liability to cover professional services that you render. These types of excluded situations would be more appropriately covered under a business owner's policy (BOP), or a commercial general liability (CGL) policy. Some policies may cover defamation, but refer to your specific policy.

Claims arising out of your employment obligations, practices and policies are excluded.

Generally, they are referring to claims made on the basis of discrimination, humiliation, harassment, or violations of federal acts such as the American's with Disabilities Act (ADA).[16] As is discussed in another section in this book, these types of claims are more appropriately covered under an employment practices liability (EPL) policy.[17]

Although these are the most common exclusions, many excluded acts or circumstances may be covered by either a separate type of policy or an endorsement. You may have fewer or a greater number of exclusions. Your insurance company will have the final say on whether and to what extent they are willing to accept additional risk and on any additional premium required to add coverage. It's worth sitting down with your broker and discussing your exclusions and whether you require additional coverage.

Chapter 6

What Minimum Limits Should I Carry?

"People who live in glass houses ... should take out insurance."
—Unknown

While the question itself is simple, the actual logic behind structuring optimal insurance protection is complicated. It requires a keen mind, an honest teacher, and quite a bit of statistical data. While we've rarely come across a CPA that wants to be underinsured and overexposed, it's been an interesting journey in educating firms on what to consider.

When it comes to determining your comfort level for insurance, it's simply not enough to ask the partners of other firms what they're paying. *Keep in mind that there are a multitude of variables that go into determining specific rates, many of which even your fellow partners are not privy to.* Indeed, the cost of insurance for two identical firms can vary by as much as 50%, if they are in different states.[1] If you would like to see all of these factors, contact your state's insurance division to request a copy of an insurer's rating guidelines.

The following are seven factors to consider as a starting point to determining your firm's minimum insurance limits:

33

What is my firm's yearly revenue?

This is a good rough estimate of where you should begin your search. Keep in mind that the below is ultimately a truncated table based upon a single insurer's client base. This chart was created by CPAs looking at what other CPAs were finding acceptable, not upon your firm's particular risk profile. Also, this table only displays *per-claim* limits and not *aggregate* limits. As you will see further, there is a very unsurprising correlation between higher firm revenues and higher per-claim limits of liability.

Firm Revenue ($)	Per-Claim Limits of Liability ($)									
	100K	250K	500K	750K	1M	2M	3M	4M	5M	>5M
< 100K	26%	46%	21%	1%	6%	6%				
100K–250K	9%	37%	35%	3%	14%	14%	1%			
250k–500K	3%	20%	34%	3%	34%	34%	1%			
500K–1M	1%	8%	24%	3%	46%	46%	3%			
1M–2M	1%	2%	10%	1%	52%	52%	9%		2%	
2M–3M			2%		38%	38%	17%	1%	5%	
3M–4M			2%		27%	27%	25%	2%	3%	
4M–5M			1%		17%	17%	34%	8%	8%	1%
5M–10M					12%	12%	32%	4%	26%	1%

Limits of liability for firms in excess of $10M limits of liability or $10M in revenue are not included. This is due to the more complex nature of their exposure or insurance structuring.[2]

Note that the largest per-claim limit an insurer will typically provide in this market is $10M.[3] Once you have the need to exceed this per-claim limit, you will need to reference the Excess Insurance section of this book.

What are my regulatory requirements?

Take a close look at what type of business you own. Is there a state or a regulatory requirement? Larger firms will generally meet the state-required minimums of insurance. Many smaller entities need to carefully examine their type of business to ensure compliance.[4] Your best resource will be your state insurance board, though often times your broker should be able to discover this information from an experienced underwriter.

What is the scope of my practice?

While two firms may have identical revenues, one may be paying more for its insurance. How is this possible? Each area of practice has been quantified over the lifespan of an experienced insurer to hold a different risk. Below is a chart containing nearly 30 years of historical claims data from a major insurance company.[5] As you can see, tax work has the highest instance of claims but the lowest severity of loss. Audit work has a lower frequency of reported claims but the highest losses. In your particular firm, which areas do you operate in?

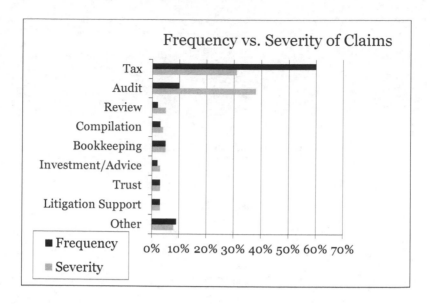

Who are my clients?

The severity of a claim can be closely related to the size and type of the client.[6] Pair this knowledge with the table shown above. Providing payroll oversight to a large business versus providing attestation services for that same business can significantly alter both the amount of coverage you should carry, as well as other internal processes in your organization. High-net-worth individuals can certainly present more exposure than the average income earner.[7] For business and personal clients, additional minimum factors to consider should be their financial solvency, their propensity for fraud, their general integrity, and industry-specific risk.[8]

Consider if you have large clients who are currently heavily leveraged or happen to be behind on payments. If anything goes wrong, you could quickly have a large contingent of disgruntled people inquiring about the services you rendered. Even fending off baseless claims can become time consuming and costly.

What are my assets?

In our opinion, this is a purely theoretical argument used to scare partners into higher insurance limits. It is well understood in insurance law that insurers are required to attempt to settle suits for their insureds within policy limits.[9] Speaking with the CEO of one of the largest insurers for CPAs in the nation, he disclosed that *he can only recall three cases in the last 30 years that exceeded policy limits.* This was primarily due to having plaintiffs with deep pockets and a personal vendetta against the CPA.[10] Indeed, a professional liability policy is specifically designed to protect your personal and firm assets from the consequences of a claim.[11]

Do my engagement letters limit my liability?

Given a claim, a properly worded engagement letter is your first line of defense.[12] Particular types of engagements may lend themselves to having engagement letters that include a limitation of liability clause.[13] This attempts to cap an award in case of litigation, usually for reimbursement of fees or some multiple of fees. This is a good number to consider purchasing for the absolute bare minimum in *per-claim* insurance. Of course, you still need to consider how to insure for defense expenses.

Finally, keep in mind that certain audit or other attest services cannot include an indemnification and limitation of liability provision, as dictated by the Indemnification and Limitation of Liability Provisions section of the AICPA Code of Conduct.[14]

Am I carrying a separate defense limit?

Separate defense limits will help pay the costs of defense in a claim before eroding your limits of liability.[15] Separate defense limits are also loosely referred to as claim expense in addition to the limit, additional limit for claim expenses, or defense outside the limit. As we have discussed before, there comes a point when you need to consider whether it is prudent to have your limits start to erode, as this might to encourage a quicker settlement.[16] Strategically, the necessity for you to purchase a separate defense limit will depend on your firm's specific engagements, your scope of business, and your per-claim and aggregate limits. Depending on your firm, you may elect to forgo a separate defense limit in favor of a higher per-claim limit. However, this is always a discussion you should have with an experienced broker and legal counsel.

Chapter 8 of this book is wholly dedicated to this topic.

———————————

We have spent almost three decades of total experience advising accounting firms on how to best position themselves with their professional insurance. However, we realize that each firm has its own distinct personality and acceptance of risk. We could show you all the available statistics, but it ultimately comes down to how well you'd like to sleep at night. At the end of the day, we are highly educated and experienced advisors, but <u>there is no policy that will keep you 100% safe.</u> *It is important to note, however, that the final decision rests in your hands based on your own comfort level.*

Chapter 7

Split Limits vs. Single Limits

"You don't need miracles in The West. You have insurance."
—Liu Zhenying

Regardless of your insurer, each policy will carry both per-claim and aggregate limits of liability. Per-claim limits refer to the amount that an insurer will absorb for a single claim.[1] The aggregate limit is how much an insurer will absorb over the course of your policy period, which is generally one year.[2] When you have a "single limit," you have an identical per-claim and aggregate limit of liability.

For many small firms, a single-limit policy of $1M per claim and $1M annual aggregate may suffice to cover the majority of situations.[3] When coupled with a $250K separate defense limit to pay defense expenses, this is a reasonable start to protecting your business. Even some small firms may need additional protection so, as always, work with a trusted broker to determine your exact needs.

As your firm grows, so will the resultant number of potential claims which could later evolve into a claim. Unfortunately, there is no magic number or set of cues that will signal you to begin looking into a more robust insurance solution. In our experience, as small firms grow they will then begin to inquire about doubling their single-limit

39

policy from a $1M/$1M to a $2M/$2M policy limit.

Regardless of firm size, when considering higher limits, begin your search by looking at a split-limit policy. Unlike a single-limit policy,[4] a split-limit policy will allow for you to have multiple losses, subject to the per-claim maximum, within a policy year.[5] For example, a $1M/$2M limit can pay out as much as two $1M claims within the year before the limits have been exhausted.

Increasing from a single limit to a split limit can be reasonable for a number of factors:

- A split-limit policy will generally mean a lesser increase in premium than an overall increase in your limits. We were recently advising a firm which had reached the point where they had outgrown their $1M/$1M policy. At their renewal, we worked with the underwriter to quote a $1M/$1M policy as a basis for comparison against a $1M/$2M policy and a $2M/$2M policy. The results? The $1M/$2M policy was only 8% more expensive than the base $1M/$1M policy, whereas the $2M/$2M policy was a full 30% more expensive over base. Why was the $1M/$2M policy only slightly more expensive?

- There is only roughly a 5% chance of the average firm receiving a claim in a policy year.[6] It would be a low probability for most small firms to receive two large claims in a policy year.

  Thus, it's a pretty safe bet for your insurer to effectively double the limits they would pay in aggregate, because the odds are very much in their favor. But why was the $2M/$2M policy so much more expensive?

- While there is only a 5% chance of having a claim in a single year,[7] remember your limits are subject to disclosure by your own insurer.[8] Having a higher single limit may increase the length and severity of litigation. While certain business practices may necessitate a higher limit to maintain accepted standards of insurance, you should always have an honest discussion with your broker to determine your exact needs. Always aim to keep your insurance limits in the "Goldilocks" zone; not too much, not too little.

This begs the question of why insurers would even offer a large single-limit policy such as a $10M/$10M, which returns us to the scope of business. If you happen to do a good amount of audit work, your chances of being sued are much lower, but the cost of defense and resultant claims are much higher.[9]

If you perform attest work for SEC clients, the risk and resultant potential claim size increases dramatically.[10] Perhaps you are engaged with a number of very high-net-worth individuals, further increasing your risk for a sizeable claim.[11] Although you can often limit damages for certain engagements based upon a carefully crafted engagement letter,[12] certain attest services cannot include an indemnification and limit of liability provision.[13] As such, costs can quickly escalate and need to be accounted for in a worst-case loss scenario.

As brokers, we can only advise you on your firm's risk profile and what you might consider as the minimum protection for your firm. Ultimately, it is your decision on whether or not you want to increase your limits and how you structure that increase.

Always remember that no policy will offer unlimited amounts of protection. Work closely with you broker, and if necessary, legal counsel familiar with claims in your profession to determine your specific needs.

Chapter 8

Separate Defense Limits

"Where there is a will … there is a lawsuit."
—Addison Mizner

Most professional liability insurers offer a separate defense limit, also known as defense outside the limits or additional limit for claim expenses. In our experience, many firms either don't fully appreciate the impact of this option or naturally assume that more insurance is better insurance.

Under a policy with *no* separate defense limit, expenses associated with your defense of a claim will erode your available limits.[1] For instance, if you have a $1M per-claim limit and incurred $500K in defense expenses, you would have $500K remaining to pay a settlement or judgement.

Generally, defense expenses include reasonable attorney fees, expert witness testimony, and investigation costs. Anyone who has ever been involved with a claim can attest that defense expenses can add up rather quickly.

If your firm elects to purchase a separate defense limit, this will give a specified amount of coverage that will apply directly towards your defense. Generally, these limits will range from $100K to $1M or even mirror your limit of liability.[2] If the defense of your claim continues after the defense limit has been exhausted, your limit of liability will begin to erode to pay additional defense expenses. Depending on your state, there may be a maximum separate defense limit allowed by law, or your insurer may have to pay all defense expenses outside your limits.

Knowing this, why would you not consider having the largest separate defense limit you could reasonably afford? The answer is much more nuanced and must be weighed with a host of other factors. Consider the following:

Psychology

Given a claim, your insurance company will likely disclose your policy limits to the plaintiff, who is probably looking to maximize their monetary return.[3] Having excessive separate defense limits may motivate the plaintiff to continue litigation if they know that your limits are remaining intact.[4]

A smaller defense limit may enable adequate defense. Be aware this could eventually erode and begin consuming your overall limits. Given prolonged litigation, this may motivate a *faster* settlement by the claimant to maximize returns.[5] A faster settlement or other resolution ultimately means that you can get back to focusing on your firm.

Your Policy

Consider what limits of liability, both per claim and aggregate, are appropriate for a firm of your size and scope of business. If in doubt, reference the previous chapter on determining appropriate limits and work with a trusted broker or legal professional familiar accountants' professional liability.

Endeavor to place your firm in the "Goldilocks" zone. Never be underinsured, or you may end up looking for a new job. Avoid being over-insured, possibly motivating a claimant to exaggerate their damages and force a higher payout after prolonged litigation.

Your Insurer

How experienced is your insurance company? As we discussed previously, having an experienced insurer with a long track record of defending your profession can be incredibly beneficial. Experienced insurers are more likely to have well-developed relationships with specified legal counsel. How responsive was your insurer to previous claims or potential claims? When notified, did they simply issue a letter of acknowledgement, or did they expertly analyze the fact pattern, walk you through the various scenarios, and provide sound advice? Non-responsive or bare-bones programs should make you question whether they have the resources to resolve your matter.

Your Clients

Consider the litigious nature and economic volatility of the industries you service. Understand that the claims frequency in insurance is closely linked with the economy.[6] Consider who you do business with, realizing that some of your clients may have backgrounds that are a red flag. Claim results point to plaintiffs having backgrounds that suggest the CPA would have never engaged had they known about previous issues. Consider performing an internet search of existing clients that you are skeptical about and, of course, all new clients. Make a decision whether to go further and invest in a background check.

When all is said and done, it becomes a balancing act between protection and leverage. Having too much insurance can encourage a lengthy and painful claim; too little and you are putting your firm at risk. Speak with your broker about the above considerations to determine comfortable defense limits. Always remain wary of "more is better."

Chapter 9

Choosing a Deductible

"I don't want to tell you how much insurance I carry with
Prudential, but all I can say is: when I go, they go."
—Jack Benny

CPAs often ask how to select an appropriate deductible. The deductible is how much you must pay out-of-pocket before your insurance company begins to pay for expenses or losses covered by your policy.[1] The higher your chosen deductible, the lower your premium, as you are essentially assuming more monetary risk, either per claim or in the aggregate. The below is a set of factors to consider when determining what deductible might be right for your firm.

What deductibles are offered?

Depending on your insurer, there may be a minimum deductible for your firm size and exposure. This is to ensure that you have "skin in the game." Certain carriers will set a minimum deductible of between 0.5% and 1% of gross revenues. Know that this percentage does vary across the marketplace.

Does your deductible apply to both claims and potential claims?

Paying out-of-pocket for all potential claims can substantially increase your deductible exposure. This can also create an adversarial environment with your insurer when you realize that your policy only truly responds to a claim, and you're on your own for every other issue. Unfortunately, failure to report a potential claim which later becomes a claim could put your coverage at risk.[2]

Ideally, your insurer pays for all expenses incurred while your matter is considered a potential claim. Be sure to identify this language in your policy. It is in the best interest of you and your insurer to invest in mitigating a matter before it evolves into a claim, if for no other reason than to keep costs down.[3] Logically, this can be deduced from the fact that some insurers offer a deductible credit for early reporting. It's not altruism on their part to offer a deductible credit, but entirely pragmatic.

Also, if potential claim expenses are covered, a higher deductible might make sense. This is especially true if your insurer has the back room necessary to help control the exposure. Remember, the back room expertise you *need* in such a situation most likely resides with the most experienced insurers in the market. They can attract and retain the most qualified experts.

If this is not in the policy language, there is no certainty in how your insurer will respond. It also may be an indication that they may not be prepared for or serious about potential claim resolution. Though you may pay more for a policy that resolves potential claims, it is certainly worth the extra upfront cost to avoid potentially larger downstream expenses and exposures.

Certain costs, such as regulatory inquiries or disciplinary proceeding expenses may have a specific sublimit. These sublimits may not be subject to your deductible and may or may not erode your overall policy limits. Once the sublimit has been exhausted, you will be responsible for all further costs. *As is often true in life, you get what you pay for.*

What is your scope of business?

As noted previously, tax work has the highest probability of a claim, while attestation has a much lower probability but tends to carry a higher ultimate cost.[4]

Consider both the potential claim frequency and severity as important variables. If you are heavy on tax work, you might consider a lower or aggregate deductible. If your focus is attestation or consulting, you might consider a higher deductible to lower your premium. This is all about managing your risk and the financial impact deductibles will have on your firm.[5]

How much risk can you afford to carry on your deductible?

Never pick so large a deductible that it would create a significant financial hardship. Insurers generally have deductible ranges for firm size. Many junior firms or sole practitioners can be enticed by a lower premium with a higher deductible but not fully appreciate their ability to afford it. Multiples of your deductible should be liquid and readily available with little, if any, impact on daily operations.

While more than one claim per year would be the exception for most firms, plan for the worst and assume that your deductible will be a yearly operating cost.[6] If after this calculation, your firm can still operate smoothly, you're on the right track. If you're a large firm, this is a conversation to have with partners at each renewal to reach a comfortable consensus. Be sure to consider the possibility of an aggregate deductible. This can be especially important with high deductibles.

Does your insurer offer a deductible credit, and to what amount?

Certain insurers often offer a deductible credit for reporting potential claims. For example, one of the stalwarts in accountants' professional liability offers a 50% deductible reduction up to $50,000 for reporting a potential claim. This feature can allow you to consider increasing your deductible, while also lowering your premium.

While this can be a very appealing option, there are a few caveats. You need to establish a culture where even the most junior employee is comfortable reporting a potential claim to management. A specialized broker should offer in-firm training to discuss loss prevention, policy compliance and what defines a potential claim. Also, you still need to ensure that this increased deductible will not bring undue financial hardship if you are not eligible for the 50% credit. With some insurers, there is a similar deductible credit for either using or resolving a claim through mediation. Reportable matters that should be discussed with your partners and staff are covered in Chapter 14.

Will you be using a Dollar One Defense (First Dollar Defense) option?

A dollar one defense option allows an insured to forgo paying their deductible for defense expenses. You opt instead to have the deductible apply to damages awarded or settlements under the policy.[7] If your insurance company pays $100K for your defense and nothing for indemnity, your firm pays nothing. In our experience, it's generally more popular with smaller firms. Dollar one defense boils down to a small monetary bet that you'll have, and win, a claim. If offered by your insurer, this option should be discussed with your partners and a knowledgeable broker.

Chapter 10

Renewing Your Professional Liability Policy

"There are worse things in life than death. Have you ever spent an evening with an insurance salesman?"

—Woody Allen

This chapter is a reference on how your renewal process should ideally function. For the purposes of brevity, your renewal date will be marked as "R." For instance, R-75 would indicate 75 days until your renewal date. These are soft dates, meaning they are subject to changes based upon your inputs, state regulations, broker efficiency and expertise, and the time of year you renew. It's worth entering the following dates on your calendar now.

Renewal Date:____/____/____

R-75:____/____/____

R-60:____/____/____

R-35:____/____/____

R-10:____/____/____

R-7:____/____/____

R-0:____/____/____

R+30:____/____/____

R-75

Reference this book with your renewal team and consider your requirements. Specifically, start thinking about new exposures or firm changes incurred since your previous renewal. Bear in mind some policies require you report certain changes during the policy year. Such mid-term reportable changes might include mergers or acquisitions, forming or selling a subsidiary, moving into financial services, adding HR consulting, becoming a receiver, other fiduciary roles, and accepting an SEC registrant or a financial institution client. Even if these changes are not required to be reported mid-term, it is recommended that you consider doing so. This will help prevent a coverage or renewability issue later.

At a minimum, have your partner group convene to discuss the below items. This will help your renewal team more efficiently build your application and help you better understand your combined risk:

- Are there any current claims or potential claims? (Reference Chapter 14, "Reportable Matters," for a convenient list.)

- Is anyone a director or officer for a client or non-client, or have an equity interest in organizations that you provide professional services to?

- Are there any new trusteeships, executorships or personal representative appointments? Are there any changes to those on file? Is anyone now a guardian, conservator or have power of attorney for a client?

- Is anyone managing, controlling, or operating a client entity? If so, know that coverage is excluded in many policies for professional services rendered. Consider entities integrated in trusts or estates for which you serve as trustee, executor or personal representative.

- Is anyone acting as a temporary or interim CFO, or as a receiver? Acting as a CFO for hire falls into, or can be easily construed as, managing controlling or operating a separate entity. If excluded by your policy, you may need to request an endorsement for coverage. Court appointed receiverships can generally be covered. Be sure to inquire about coverage when a receivership is not court appointed, as these are heavily scrutinized.

- Is anyone disbursing client funds outside of a fiduciary role? This might include paying bills for a client or making wire transfers. Some policies provide a sublimit of liability, for your staff misappropriating client funds.

It's worth referencing the additional coverage options listed in this book: employment practices liability, cyber, RIA, D&O, and excess policies. Begin the discussion on whether you may need a proposal for these additional coverage areas. You can always obtain a proposal for these policies for consideration. Communicate your intentions to your broker to review these options.

R-60

You should have your renewal application(s) now in hand. Inquire about new or changed application questions, emerging insurer concerns, or changes to the policy or program. Be prepared to answer all questions fully and provide explanations to help clarify your exposure. Failure to provide an answer can later result in unforeseen and unnecessary headaches.[1] It is safe to say that you should answer every single question, even with an N/A. Answering "Yes" to certain questions may require a "supplemental application." Getting an early start, particularly to uncover any required supplements, will help make your renewal smoother.

Also, have no qualms about calling or meeting with your broker to speak about your questions or concerns. Armed with the information in this book, you will undoubtedly be well ahead of your peers with loss prevention and insurance knowledge.

If you are looking for multiple proposals, you may have to fill out additional applications. Depending on the relationship your current broker has with the market, he may or may not have the ability to propose different insurers or types of policies. In the strictest sense, "captive agents" can only offer insurance from one company, whereas brokers will have multiple offerings.[2] Be incredibly wary of random discount insurers offering a "soft" or "preliminary" quote. A perennial favorite of drive-by salesmen is the email that compares your current insurer to their insurer with a lower quote. Nearly without exception, we find they're filled with misleading or incorrect information. Saving money with a policy that doesn't adequately cover your exposures is not advised. Focus on what problems you are trying to solve, and you'll be ahead of the game.

When in doubt, we recommend you ask the broker the "Four Simple Questions" and reference Chapter 2, "Warning Signs." If it suits you, you always have the option of comparing true policy specifics using Chapter 4, "Professional Liability Insurance Policy Specifics," as a guideline.

R-35

This is when you should have transmitted your application to your broker. At this point, your broker will review your application, and ask for any clarifications. Your broker will send off your application to your underwriter, who will then quantify your risks and formulate renewal terms.

R-10/14

If you have met all of your timelines, this is when you should have your renewal proposal. Look very closely at the specimen policy language, as well as the terms of coverage and limits being offered. Speak with your broker about your specific risks and business plans. Inquire if the proposed policy will provide appropriate solutions. We also recommend that you reference the chapters in this book dealing with your specific renewal options: "Split Limits vs. Single Limits," "Choosing a Deductible," and "What Minimum Limits Should I Carry."

Keep in mind that part of your premium will be based on market trends, even down to the litigation history in your geographic area.[3] The bad news is you can't control all variables, and your rate may have an adjustment regardless of your diligence. The good news is your specific areas of practice, or the market in general, may be trending rates in your favor. Either way, you're dealing with an insurer that is keeping tabs on the litigation tendencies in your specific area, which is a good thing.

R-7

This is when you should email *and* mail your insurance order to your broker.[4] Understand the premium payment requirements, as the timing of premium payment will vary by broker and insurer. Having an extra few days in reserve will let your broker and insurer work with you on any additional questions or concerns. Be sure to reference the "Prior to Bind" section in your proposal, which may request additional information. Responses to these requirements could change the terms and conditions of the proposal.

Most likely, your policy will be a "claims made and reported" policy.[5] Speak with firm owners and all staff to discover any information or knowledge of any act, error, omission, fact, situation, circumstance, or unresolved dispute which has already resulted in a demand for money or service; or, anything which might reasonably be expected to give rise to a claim. This might include, but is not limited to, a known error, ethics allegations, regulatory inquiry, restatement or reissuance, receipt of a subpoena, problems with the IRS, cease and desist orders, whistle-blower situation, expected client demand, damage to a client network, compromise of client information, deepening insolvency or bankruptcy, discovery of a fraud or Ponzi scheme, third-party request for client information, tax penalty (all are technically reportable), request to sign a tolling agreement, disengagement due to adverse circumstances, adverse information in the media about a client, request from a third party to sign a reliance letter, or disciplinary action or investigation by a court, board or regulatory agency.

Failure to disclose a potential claim before your renewal date can result in a declination of coverage should a matter later become a claim.[6]

An insurer declining to offer renewal terms for your next policy period is usually exposure driven, meaning they suspect constant, systemic risk in your firm. Reporting a potential claim should not normally result in a non-renewal scenario. When in doubt: *Disclose, Disclose, Disclose.* A slight bump in premium is always better than no coverage at all.

Waiting until the last day to order coverage is stressful and potentially hazardous to your business. Last-minute deadlines open you up to a lapse of coverage. It can also limit your ability to work with your broker to minimize your business exposures. Most CPAs don't know that their policy actually expires at 12:01 AM on the day of your renewal, not midnight of that renewal day. *Always plan ahead* to avoid unnecessarily creating a dangerous situation for your firm.

R-Day

This is when your coverage should be "bound."[7] This means that your new policy goes into effect on your renewal date for the next policy period. Also, your policy limits should refresh. Should you be enticed by a two-year policy term, be sure to understand whether the limit refreshes at the halfway point.

If you'd like evidence of coverage, request a binder. This serves as a temporary contract of insurance until you are delivered the policy.[8] Keep in mind that each insurer and state have a maximum number of days that they will provide coverage without full payment. Some insurers may require that your policy be fully funded by your renewal date. If you are financing your premium, work with your broker to confirm that you are in compliance with all your specific financing terms.

R+30

By this point you should have a policy in hand.[9] Double check that your exact order has been met. Specifically, check your policy for the limits and terms you requested from your broker, and confirm all of your endorsements are in order.

This is also a good time to train employees on policy benefits and responsibilities. Good insurers and stellar brokers will offer year-round employee and partner training opportunities on policy specifics and loss prevention. Receiving a policy is not the finish line; we would recommend you reference Chapter 11, "PLI -Now What?" to get the most from your new policy and insurer.

Why you should never cut it close:

Always submit your renewal application and renewal order with plenty of time to spare. Occasionally, CPAs will push their renewal process to the very last second. Unbeknownst to most CPAs, a lapse in coverage can have serious ramifications for your business. It can leave you with years, sometimes decades, of business activity that is not covered. If you fail to obtain an extension or renew on time, you may have to consider an extended reporting period (ERP) endorsement:

- After policy expiration, you will likely have an automatic ERP[10] of approximately 30 to 60 days to report any known claims that were made during your policy period.

- You will also likely have the option to buy an ERP endorsement (tail policy). This option is usually available up to 30 days after your policy has expired. If you do not purchase a tail, you will no longer have coverage for prior acts. The specifics of this type of policy are covered in detail later in the book. All costs, penalties, fines, and rulings from a claim not covered will be paid out of your own pocket. Recall that 97% of claims occur within seven years of work completion,[11] and that the cost of defense can be substantial. Referencing your policy, you will see that a tail policy will often cost upwards of 200% of your current policy premium, depending on insurer and length of tail. Reference Chapter 12, "Extended Reporting Periods – Tail Policies," for more specifics.

If you miss your renewal, you will need to scramble to find a new insurance policy, which can be stressful and time consuming. As part of this process, you will also need to ensure that your new policy provides all of the specific coverages that your firm requires.

Also, the new insurer may not provide any coverage for your lapsed prior acts. Like all other businesses, insurance companies are weary of dealing with clients who have had a policy lapse. Indeed, many new insurance applications will ask about a retroactive date limitation on your existing policy, providing additional headaches for years to come if you decide to switch carriers. You will likely have a new retroactive date that begins when your new policy is bound.

Chapter 11

PLI – Now What?

"The muse honors the working stiff."

—Steven Pressfield

Y ou wouldn't just hire an employee, send them a large check once a year and let them operate in a complete vacuum, would you? Once you've gone through all the steps from the previous chapters, take full advantage of your hard work. It's time that all of the effort that you put into the relationship with your broker and insurer be reciprocated.

At a minimum, we recommend you work with your broker and insurer to review the following points. Your broker and insurer should welcome the discussion, offering additional services at no extra charge. Once completed, we recommend that you stay engaged with your loss prevention measures throughout the year. Continue to report claims, subpoenas, regulatory inquiries, potential claims, and changes in your practice to your insurer, via your broker.

Your document retention policy

Experienced insurers will be able to provide technical recommendations on your document retention policy. At an absolute minimum, your document retention policy should consider what to keep and for how long. Sources for inclusion in your policy can include faxes, emails, images, electronic working papers, and physical documents. Don't forget to compare your preferences with legal requirements, such as statute of limitation laws, discovery rules, filing requirements, and the rules of your state accountancy board.[1] Also, consider the method of storage; hard-drives are cheap but can lose data over time due to bit-rot, magnetic tapes are more secure and lose much less data over long periods of time.[2] Likely, your insurer will have sample retention policies that you could implement with some modifications, to meet your specific requirements.

Your existing and new client evaluation process

It's helpful to have a system, if not an explicit written policy, to deal with client evaluation.[3] This can help focus your practice on attracting and maintaining quality clients, while potentially keeping you out of bad situations. Ensuring even the most junior accountant is aware of certain red flags will also allow for more streamlined communication and eliminate ambiguity in the ranks.

Your insurer should have standardized checklists that you can modify to form a basis for your own system.

Your engagement and disengagement letters

Your letters should be implemented throughout your entire practice and be amended to account for engagement creep. Basic engagement letters should clearly define the scope of work, how fees will be charged, and other terms such as ending date, client responsibility, and alternative dispute resolution.[4] Besides having letters that are compliant with a peer review process, recall that your engagement letter is your first line of defense. Having letters that are current with the latest trends and legal rulings are invaluable.[5]

When a disengagement letter is being sent, most often there is already a problem. Common issues include unsubstantiated positions on tax returns, conflicts of interest, or fundamental struggles on a personal and professional level.[6] For this reason, it is important to ensure they are updated and reviewed at least annually.

Your insurer or a legal professional familiar with the field should be able to assist in drafting engagement or disengagement letters for nearly any situation.

Have your website and marketing material reviewed for liability issues

As the world becomes more connected, websites have become a necessity for conducting business, marketing your expertise and providing useful information. Inadvertently providing legal advice or improper disclaimers can open your practice up to unnecessary litigation.[7] There is a fine line between marketing and professional advice.

Have your insurer review your site initially and then again with any changes. Working with legal counsel to develop effective disclaimers will also help address the grey area that often occurs, especially with blogging and content marketing.

Utilize your insurer's tax review services

Your insurer may have a team of in-house JD/CPAs to provide free comment on complex or technical tax issues, as well as tax abatement strategies.[8] All tax penalties are likely considered to be a reportable matter to your insurer. While a common practice, consider that paying a penalty on your own without insurer consent means that you are assuming liability.[9]

Under your policy, you very likely have a clause that states that you can't settle matters without your insurer's consent. By doing so you may forfeit all insurer protection. If you look inside your professional liability policy, you will likely have a clause similar to the following:

> "The Insured will not, except at the Insured's own cost, voluntarily make any payment of Claims Expenses or Damages, assume or admit any liability, or incur any Claims Expenses or other expenses without the prior written consent of the Company."[10]

Take advantage of free CPE

Most insurers offer varying levels of CPE. Some are quite robust, with 20 or more hours in various subjects available for all staff. Some programs are even offered at no additional charge. These CPE credits can come in many forms: webcasts, self-study, and in-house group or off-site presentations. Surprisingly, many firms will forget that this cost saving measure is a benefit of their program.

Have your insurer review your government contracts

While often low-margin engagements, the government will (almost always) pay you on time and in full. However, there can be a number of strict requirements.[11] If you are dealing frequently in this area, it is all too easy to have hold-harmless agreements, certain indemnity clauses, and other strict requirements slip past you. Avoid the possibility of having no coverage or recourse by having these contracts reviewed by professionals. Don't potentially sign away your policy's effectiveness and protections.

Chapter 12

Extended Reporting Periods/Tail Policies (M&A)

"This really is a merger of equals. I wouldn't have come back to work for anything less than this fantastic opportunity. This lets me combine my two great loves – technology and biscuits."

—Lou Gerstner

ergers and acquisitions are always a hot topic for CPAs. As more CPAs are preparing for retirement, firms are actively acquiring the client bases that these firms possess. One important consideration with these transactions is how professional liabilities will be handled following the transaction.[1]

Once you have retired, you certainly don't want to deal with a claim or potential claim when you would rather be pursuing other interests. If you're the one acquiring another firm, you've likely had no oversight on the quality of work or client screening processes of the practice you purchased. This also holds true in a merger situation.

To manage these exposures, policies generally offer an extended reporting period (ERP) option, also known as a tail policy.[2] This provides coverage for *claims that occur after your professional liability insurance has ended, for work that occurred during the policy period.*[3] Essentially, claims arising from professional services rendered from your policy retroactive date through the end of your last active policy are covered in an elected tail policy period. Most policies do include an automatic ERP. This allows claims already made prior to the expiration of the policy to be reported 30 to 60 days after the policy has expired.

Remember that 97% of claims typically occur within seven years of work *completion.*[4] As such, consider selecting the longest tail period offered. Insurers usually offer tail policy periods of one, three, five, or seven years. For a seven-year policy, you can expect to pay 200%+ of your current policy premium. Some insurers will offer an unlimited option, but this means that they are agreeing to keep reserves on hand *forever* in case of a claim. Expect to see only an unlimited option from transient insurers, or unless required by your state.

With the sizeable cost of defending even a baseless claim, a firm should be very aware of selecting the appropriate tail period. This is a one-time decision that can have serious implications on your firm and the success of acquisitions and mergers. We are unaware of any third-party tail policies for purchase to renew an expiring tail policy period. Once you make your decision, you're stuck with it.

Below are tail policy fundamentals to consider prior to purchasing a tail policy:

1. Report all claims and potential claims prior to purchasing a tail policy. Failure to report these matters before you purchase a tail policy could later result in a declination of coverage.[5]

2. When a merger or acquisition is completed, an engagement letter should be issued to clients of the merged or acquired firm. This serves the purpose of clearly defining the date when the work (and liability) of the newly combined firm begins and when the liability of the merged or acquired firm ends.

3. The premium you pay to your insurer for an ERP (tail policy) is fully earned when it is bound; it cannot be financed or later canceled.

4. This is a one-time decision. Changes to the tail cannot be made later.

5. Unlike your professional liability policy, your limits do not refresh every year. The limits you purchase can be exhausted throughout your ERP. If you are aware of a later need for a tail, consider increasing your limits at your renewal.

6. The terms and conditions of your existing policy apply to your tail policy. Your tail policy is an endorsement which applies to your existing policy; understand it well.

7. Ideally, you should begin working with your broker and insurer one year or more in advance to consider limit adequacy and policy language particulars.

8. Consider seeking advice from legal counsel in concert with your broker about the length and policy language of a tail policy.

9. Consider purchasing the longest tail policy possible. Remember that 97% of claims occur within seven years of work completion.[6] The cost of additional coverage per year decreases as a percentage of overall premium.

10. <u>Once a tail policy expires, you will no longer have any coverage.</u>

What if your firm is doing individual tax returns only? The general rule for the IRS on the assessment of taxes expires three years from the due date or filing of the return.[7] Shouldn't you just buy a three-year policy? Not exactly.

Recall that the IRS actually has a six-year statute if they believe there has been a substantial omission (greater than 25%) on the return of gross income.[8] Also, there is an indefinite statute if they believe there has been a false or fraudulent return, a willful attempt to evade tax, or a failure to file a return.[9] In these instances, it is entirely plausible that your firm's client was at fault, and that it was completely outside the realm of knowledge or control for that firm. The firm may still have vicarious liability or just get wrapped up in a baseless claim. Don't put your practice retirement, merger, or acquisition at risk.

Now that we understand the basics of a tail policy, let's discuss the three most common types of M&A scenarios and how a tail policy fits into each.

Scenario 1 – Acquisition: Large (L) + Small (S) = Bigger (B)

Large firm (L) acquires or merges with Smaller firm (S), creating Bigger firm (B). Smaller firm purchases a tail policy. Larger firm brings in Smaller firm's client base and possibly the personnel.

- In this scenario, (S) has purchased a tail policy and (L) is not responsible for the prior acts of (S). Any claims or potential claims arising out of the work of (S), from retroactive date through the termination of their practice's policy, will be covered under the tail policy of (S).

- (B) is able to continue with its previous policy when it was (L). The new personnel from (S) are included as insureds, for new services rendered from the transaction date, under the policy of (B).

- (L) may still have some vicarious liability by being associated with (S). If a potential claim or claim is to arise, (B) may incur defense costs to disassociate itself from the issue arising from the work of (S).

- On the date of acquisition, your insurer may request an additional premium for the additional exposure. Insurers commonly consider the volume and type of work, as well as the amount of time remaining on the policy.

- Large Firm (L) should revisit their policies to consider increased revenue, personnel and exposures.

Scenario 2 – Merger: (A) + (B) = (AB)

Firm (A) merges with Firm (B) to create Firm (AB). Usually, the larger of the two firms will be able to continue their current policy. This requires prior insurer approval. Firm (B) is named as an insured under Firm (A)'s policy, with (B)'s retroactive date honored on an endorsement. In this scenario, both firms (A) and (B) are covered under (A)'s policy. Neither (A) nor (B) purchases a tail policy.

- Any future claim made against the work of (A) or (B) will now be considered under the policy of firm (AB).

- Any future claim against the work completed by (A) or (B) can deplete the limits of liability for (AB).

- (AB) should consider increasing their limits of liability for all policies to account for their increased scale and exposure.

- The total coverage cost for (AB) will be larger than the premium for either (A) or (B), but there may be some economies of scale.

- As (B) is endorsed on (A)'s policy, there may be a limit of liability restriction. (B)'s prior acts coverage may be limited to the limit they carried on their previous policy.

Scenario 3 – Creation: (A) + (B) = (C)

Firm (A) and Firm (B) combine to create a new entity, Firm (C). In this scenario, both firms (A) and (B) purchase a tail policy. Firm (C) begins work with a new policy and a retroactive date at policy inception.

- Both (A) and (B) have purchased tail policies. The work completed during their time as individual firms will be covered under their respective tail policies. These tail policies will likely have a finite coverage period. Unlike a continuous policy, those prior acts will, at a certain point, no longer have coverage. This is, of course, if neither purchased an unlimited tail policy.

- Should a claim arise from the work of (A) or (B), (C) will likely have vicarious liability to defend against. This can become a challenging liability to insure against.

- (C)'s first policy should account for the increased personnel and liability exposure in their new practice. The firm should consider increasing their limits of liability beyond what either (A) or (B) had individually prior to the merger.

Each merger or acquisition is structured differently and is unique to the circumstances of the firms coming together. Work with your broker to consider what options are available, and their respective benefits and consequences.

M&A checklist

We have provided a checklist of items for you to consider carefully. Along with your legal counsel and a knowledgeable insurance broker, these can prove helpful before a merger or acquisition. Consider this checklist a starting point, as there may be many other issues to contemplate.

Culture comparison

- What is the standard work attire of the other firm (tie or no tie)? Does it match yours?
- What are the average billable hours per professional?
- What is their culture of customer service?
- Is customer satisfaction or the bottom line more important? Does this match your view?
- How are employee issues handled?
- Does the firm have a functioning loss prevention culture?
- Is there a quality control partner?
- Has there been a recent EQCR? What were the findings?
- Have there been recent terminations or key employees/partners who have left the firm?
- Does the firm have an HR professional or division? What specific benefits does each employee receive? Are these policies current with local, state, and federal laws? Are they compatible with your firm's policies?
- Is the firm or any firm member currently under investigation by any boards, societies, or regulators?
- How does the firm handle CPE?
- Does the firm belong to any AICPA Practice Sections (i.e. PCPS,

GAQC, EBPAQC, CAQ)?

- What is the current financial situation of the firm?
- Obtain the full peer review report to include MFCs and discuss any findings to include remediation.

Liability history inquiry

- Obtain at least a five-year "loss run" on the firm. All insurance brokers will be familiar with this term. This will document any past and pending claims from their most recent insurer. If they have switched carriers recently, have them request a loss run from their previous insurers, as well.

- Do they have any pending issues which could later result in a claim or potential claim? Have these or will these be reported?

- Have there been any complaints to, or actions taken by, any board or regulatory agency? This should include SEC, DOL, PCAOB, state societies, AICPA, etc.

- Does the firm utilize engagement and disengagement letters?
- Obtain previous disengagement letters used and discuss the reasons for disengagement.

- What types of insurance do they carry? Include limits of liability, separate defense limits, and additional endorsements. A knowledgeable broker should be able to assist you in determining any additional exposures you may be taking on.

- How will liability for prior acts be covered? Will you require them to purchase a tail policy, or will they merge their prior act's liability onto your policy? Will your current insurer agree to this?

Business considerations

- What quality of clients does the firm possess? What is their cash conversion cycle?

- How does their billing rate compare to yours? Will a disparity cause a problem with clients?

- What area of practice does this firm possess that you do not? Do you feel comfortable taking on this new area?

- Does the firm continually screen clients for potential risks, late payments, or incomplete information?

- How will overlapping areas of practice be consolidated and supervised?

- How will non-overlapping work be reviewed and supervised?

- Are the non-overlapping areas of practice riskier than your current practice?

- Has the staff size increased ± 25% over the past three years?

- Have the firm's service areas shifted within the past three years?

- Is the firm a member of any national or international CPA groups or associations?

- Does the firm, or any firm member, control or distribute client funds?

- Has the firm provided services for financial institutions or SEC registrants?

- Does the firm provide services to any entities under the guidelines of ERISA?

- Does the firm provide any services as a CFO or C-Suite executive for hire?

Professional Liability Loss Prevention

Chapter 13

The Top Five Ways to Get Sued

"Fun is like insurance; the older you get the more it costs."
—Kin Hubbard

For over 25 years representing CPAs, we have noted that many claims have the same underlying problems. While the below summary is by no means a comprehensive list, most accountants' claims we've seen can be narrowed down to five general categories.

Suing your clients to collect fees

Every CPA firm has a client who either outright refuses or is otherwise unable to pay for professional services rendered. While a natural reaction of anyone is to sue to collect a fee, we nearly always advise against it.

Lawyers agree that a suit to recoup fees will substantially increase your risk for a malpractice counter-suit.[1] Counter-suits are a defendant's best avenue for a resolution. This quickly accelerates the potential costs for your firm and is a common defense tactic. The idea is to make the total cost of litigation outweigh the fees that you are trying to recoup, making the lawsuit a battle of wills.[2]

In a worst-case scenario, you will not only lose your case after substantial costs, but you will also be forced to defend against a claim. Sometimes they are baseless, others may have legitimate allegations. The suit and counter-suit will almost always result in your firm spending more money in attorney's fees and lost billable hours than you would recoup for owed fees.[3]

Also, you may actually draw a valid claim, requiring a vigorous, time consuming, and expensive defense. No matter which side of a lawsuit you are on, it's going to be an uphill battle. As a certified professional, you will always carry the burden of proof with a jury. Except in very specific circumstances, it is almost always preferable to avoid litigation over unpaid bills.

In terms of insurance, most seasoned insurers are all too familiar with counter-suit tactics. Insurers may offer your firm a direct or indirect premium credit for not suing clients to collect fees.[4] The direct premium credit often comes with the caveat that you will have no coverage if a counter-suit arises from a suit to collect fees. Even without agreeing to this credit, some insurers may require notification before attempting to sue a client for fees. Check with your insurer for your specific policy benefits and responsibilities.

Advising both parties to a transaction

Due to the inherent need for impartiality in your occupation, advising both parties to a transaction is inherently dangerous. If, for instance, you determine the depreciation value of a business and then advise a purchasing agent on those same values, you may setting yourself up for a claim. This could possibly come from both parties.

With a conflict of interest present, it is all too easy for a business to claim collusion between you and the opposing party. Furthermore, certain attest services outright require independence.[5] Never place yourself in a situation where that independence could even remotely be considered impaired, or you may quickly find yourself in a claim.

Participating in business deals with clients

It is not only a potential conflict of interest to participate in a deal with a client, but it can also be a significant liability. Whether you intend to enter the deal with your business entity or as a private individual, we always recommend against it. A jury will always assume you to be the subject-matter expert, hence, you will be starting from a position of weakness. While it is tempting to participate in a potentially lucrative business deal in the event of a sudden depreciation of assets, failure of the business, or even a market downturn, you may be opened up to a claim.

Furthermore, your insurance policy may outright deny coverage for claims that arise from this scenario. Read your policy carefully. It probably has a clause that excludes coverage for services rendered if you manage, control, or operate a non-endorsed entity. Also, any entity in which you have an ownership interest (normally 10% to 20%) is usually excluded from coverage.

Remember that your employees are also covered under your policy. As a result, those same exclusions will also apply to them. If they happen to be doing pro-bono returns for local non-profits, for instance, these services may not be covered and could get them into trouble. It is also advisable to steer clear of encouraging family members to invest in a client's business. This could easily be construed as an ethics violation by a professional ethics committee.[6]

Not communicating with clients in writing

This can cover a number of different areas, such as engagement and disengagement letters, a change in contract for services rendered, or the discovery of fraud. When you do have a significant event that could potentially result in a claim later, you should always have evidence of written communication. Without this, a suit or conflict could later devolve into a he-said-she-said argument.[7] When a claim occurs, you're going to want and need defensive documentation.

If you are caught off guard by a client phone call, always follow up with a written communication to summarize the conversation and reinforce important points. When in doubt, send a letter by certified mail, in addition to email, marking both as "sent by courier and email" to highlight the importance.

Remember that verified communications can be used as evidence; discussions are up to interpretation and potentially faulty memories.

Mistaking adherence to professional standards as a substitute for "getting it right"

All CPAs are subject to the standards of their profession, but we all understand that you can't codify every potential situation. Even though you may have done everything within the letter of the law, you can still be held liable for the outcome.[8]

In a courtroom, it may be all too easy to sway a juror with an emotional decision over rote adherence to tax law passages. A jury has the benefit of hindsight, and you, as a certified professional, are expected to "get it right" regardless of services rendered.[9] If you didn't advise your clients on every aspect of a risk and how to avoid them, or don't have proof in writing, you will likely be held accountable.

Whatever your professional choices, make sure that you are acting in accordance with your policy obligations, and that your clients have a clear understanding of your service engagement.

When in doubt, speak with a trusted broker, and seek legal counsel. Well established insurers will likely have in-house counsel who have seen your circumstance multiple times and can provide expert guidance. This alone is worth the extra cost of using an experienced insurer.

Chapter 14

Reportable Matters

"The trick is to stop thinking of it as 'your' money."
—IRS auditor

We all understand that a small fender-bender is probably not worth reporting to your insurance company. After all, for a relatively minor repair, your premium may rise in a manner disproportionate to the out-of-pocket cost. Unfortunately, we meet many CPAs who believe the same for their professional liability insurance. Professional liability insurance policies require that you report all claims and potential claims before the end of the policy period or extended reporting period. There is usually a 30 to 60 day automatic extended reporting period for this requirement. This allows you to report a claim already made against you within the 30 to 60 day window following policy expiration.

As a matter of great importance, reporting any and all claims and potential claims to your insurer early serves two purposes:

1. It will preserve your policy rights by reporting in the specified period.[1]

2. It will enable an experienced insurer to advise you on reducing your liability, attempt resolution before the issue becomes more expensive, and, if necessary, appoint appropriate defense counsel.[2]

Understanding of these purposes is invariably followed by the question, "*What* should we report?" To answer this, you need to be familiar with the difference between a claim and a potential claim.

In our experience, most CPA firms have *at least* one potential claim per year that should be reported, but most are honestly unaware. This means, unfortunately, most CPA firms across the nation are putting themselves at risk of a coverage declination by not reporting within the designated time period.[3]

Most policies require firms to give notice as soon as they have information which could reasonably invoke the coverages in their policy.[4] Your professional liability policy will contain a clause similar to the one below:

> "Insured's Duty to Report Claims Made During the Policy Period: As a condition precedent to coverage under this policy, a Claim must be reported to the Company as soon as practicable during the Policy Period …"[5]

Certainly those are vague terms, and they have been subject to numerous debates that have come to varying, sometimes conflicting, conclusions.[6] However, there is no reason to subject your coverage to doubt over policy nuances. **When in doubt, report.**

To better clarify, we have compiled a list of common potential claims for accounting firms, though by no means is it a comprehensive list:

Known error
Ethics allegations
Regulatory inquiry
Receipt of a subpoena

Problems with the IRS

Cease and desist orders

Expected client demand

Whistle-blower situation

Restatement or reissuance

Damage to a client network

Compromise of client information

Deepening insolvency or bankruptcy

Discovery of a fraud or Ponzi scheme

Tax penalty (all are technically reportable)

Third-party request for client information

Disengagement due to adverse circumstances

Adverse information in the media about a client

Request from a third party to sign a reliance letter

Disciplinary action or investigation by a court, board or regulatory agency

Any situation that you feel could bring rise to a claim

Once again, when in doubt, report, and report immediately.

A claim is most often defined in your professional liability policy as:

- any demand for money or services
- any situation that could reasonably be expected to bring rise to a claim.

Again, when in doubt, report, and report immediately.

Some examples of a potential claim could be watching a client ignore your advice as they edge closer to insolvency, or a report in a local news report which names your client in connection with a criminal investigation (adverse media report). Another example would include a divorce attorney requesting client information or receiving a subpoena.

A claim scenario might include a client demanding you "make it right" after a tax penalty, or a client demanding you pay him back for the time he lost dealing with your firm.

It is imperative that you do not offer to negotiate a settlement or admit liability without insurer approval. If you do, you will likely void your policy on the matter. As a firm, you are paying good money for coverage. Don't let it go to waste.

Well established insurers actually encourage early reporting.[7] Your broker and insurer should prompt you at each renewal to report any claims or potential claims prior to the end the policy period. It's usually less expensive for both your firm and the insurer to head off potential claims before they become actual claims.[8]

Perhaps a client is asking you to pay a $10,000 tax penalty, and your deductible is $15,000. You might just assume that you should pay the penalty to resolve the matter. This can be problematic.[9] Paying the claim yourself will probably deny you future coverage with issues related to that client and problem.[10] You will not have the benefit of insurer expertise to manage the problem.

Also, you've likely missed obtaining the appropriate releases, and you will not receive the credit towards your deductible, if offered by your insurer. By settling without insurer's consent, you're setting an expensive precedent within your firm.

It's simply much safer and easier to notify your insurer. The matter will likely then fall under coverage, and you'll have the guidance you need. With disclosure, you can expect a release form from your insurer.

This form will seek to close the matter and prohibit the client from pursing further action on the matter.

Now that you know what to look for and when to report it, take a hard look at your company culture. Are your employees encouraged to report the problems listed above? Are they even aware that this is a requirement to ensure coverage under your company's policy? Is there both a formal and informal system of reporting codified within your firm? If there is any doubt, consider providing the list of claims and potential claims to all staff or finding any innovative way to regularly communicate this information to everyone. That small investment might just save you a lot of time and effort later on. It will also encourage employees to consider the firm's best long-term interests more often.

Whenever you renew your policy you will likely sign a clause stating that no officer, director, partner, shareholder, or employee is aware of any potential claims or claims that have not been reported to your insurer. This has been referenced earlier as a claims made and reported style policy.[11] If a claim later occurs that you or any of your employees had knowledge of, your insurer has grounds to deny you coverage on that claim, and you're on your own.[12]

If you have a covered claim, many insurers will issue you a deductible credit for successful resolution through mediation. Consider an insurer that is proactive about helping you early on and offer a deductible credit for simply reporting a potential claim.

This credit might also extend to simply using mediation to attempt resolution, regardless of outcome. A seasoned insurer understands, if for no other reason than economics, that assisting your firm to find a quick resolution is almost always less expensive than going to court or hoping you figure it out on your own.[13]

Keep in mind that these credits may be worthless if you do not have a mediation clause already in your engagement letter. Certain types of engagement conflicts may be better handled through arbitration, while others are best handled through mediation. Be sure to seek advice on their relative strengths and weaknesses.[14] An experienced insurer will have sound recommendations and can tailor your engagement letters to your specific requirements.

Chapter 15

The Fundamentals of Fraud

"If at first you don't succeed ... take the tax loss."
—Kirk Kirkpatrick

Fraud is a larger problem than most CPA firms and their clients are aware of.[1] As a trusted business partner, advising your clients on their fraud exposures should be the cornerstone of your loss prevention measures.

Fraud claims tend to follow the economy. When the market is on an upswing, businesses tend to have a larger influx of money and are much less likely to notice missing funds.[2] When the market invariably turns and available capital becomes scarcer, your client will begin to look more closely at their accounts.[3]

Even as a trusted advisor, these market fluctuations will often make your job more difficult. When money is flowing, your clients will be more likely to spend their efforts on networking, sales, and marketing than scrutinizing their balance sheet. This is precisely why you should always be proactive and consistent on advising your clients on the risks of fraud.

The Association of Certified Fraud Examiners is possibly the best resource for fraud trends and statistics. Here are some key findings from their *Report to the Nations on Occupational Fraud and Abuse:*[4]

- The typical organization loses 5% of revenues each year to fraud.

- The average amount of time from fraud commencement to detection is 18 months.

- Anti-Fraud controls, such as an anonymous hotline, reduce fraud losses by 41%, and duration by 50%.

- Misappropriation causes a median loss of $130,000.

- Financial statement fraud has a median loss of $1,000,000.

- Corruption schemes have a median loss of $200,000.

When it comes to big claims, it should come as no surprise that fraud leads the pack on the severity of damages awarded.[5] When we look at the instances of fraud claims by engagement type for CPAs from one of the nation's largest CPA insurers, we see a common trend:[6]

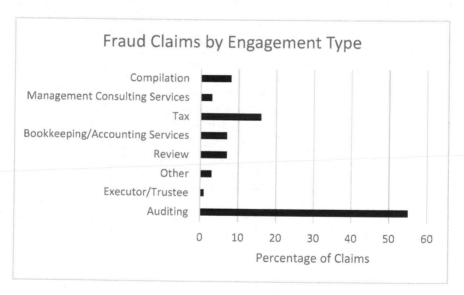

Most fraud claims come from an audit engagement, but that should come as no surprise. *Do not be lulled into a sense of security by this chart.* Juries, as well as the public at large, will expect you to detect fraud, even during non-attest engagements.[7] The longer that you provide services to your client and the greater the scope of those engagements, the more likely you will have been expected to uncover a fraud.

Do not limit your scrutiny to one class of client. While you would assume that large clients would have the highest loss ratio, due to bureaucratic complexity, it's actually small businesses which are taking the most losses.[8] As a CPA, the majority of your clients probably fall into this higher-risk, small-business category. Upon inspection, you will often see small businesses lacking even rudimentary anti-fraud controls. We recommend you consider advising all of your clients on basic anti-fraud measures. As always, failure to document your recommendations to clients can drastically weaken your legal defense.[9]

We have broken these client-focused considerations into three broad categories: general business practices, employee practices, and employee red flags.

1. General Business Practices:

- Separate the accounting and bookkeeping duties amongst at least three different people.
- Have the owner receive checks and statements unopened, directly from the bank with no middleman.
- Pay attention to customer feedback. Trends of late or missing items can be a first sign of potential fraud.
- The business owner should personally verify the vendor names and transactions.
- Avoid using signature stamps and electronic signatures.

- Require double verification of checks and deposits above a certain amount.

- Strictly limit access to blank checks. If necessary, eliminate checks entirely.

- Have the business owner conduct regular inspections for missing checks and generally suspicious activity.

- Make it a point to aggressively investigate all allegations of fraud.

- Create and enforce a zero-tolerance approach to fraud.

- Urge the business owner to utilize an independent review of cash and bank statements by anti-fraud specialists.

- Large companies may benefit from an internal audit and investigation unit.

- Institute a fraud payroll program to control payment distributions.

- Develop and communicate high ethical standards to your employees, and enforce them.

2. Employee Practices:

- Insist that employees dealing with funds take regular vacations, and conduct an independent and thorough review of their practices while they're absent.

- Consider using an employee application and request consent to conduct background and credit checks[10] and a drug test.[11] This goes a long way to eliminating problems before they become employees. Check with your HR representative to make sure this is compliant with your applicable employment laws.

- Consider screening all new potential employees for previous criminal activities. This can be done with online automated services or general internet searches. You'd be surprised how often this would have kept a company out of trouble. Ensure that it is done in accordance with state and federal laws.[12]

- Create a system for employees to anonymously report potential fraud, reward reporters, and make all employees aware of the consequences of participating in fraud.[13]

A sample of the most common Employee Behavior Red Flags, as reported by the ACFE in their *Report to the Nations on Occupational Fraud and Abuse*:[14]

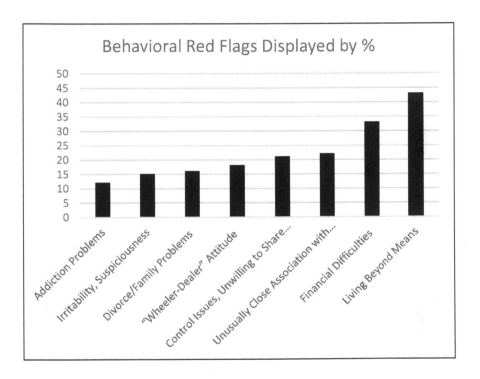

Figures do not add up to 100% due to truncated table.

On a final note, it's worth mentioning that even the most robust anti-fraud-inclined clients can still fall victim to fraud. Even if they can't prevent fraud, they can minimize its effects in terms of both time and money. For instance, rewarding whistle-blowers reduced the cost of fraud by nearly 26% and reduced the duration of fraud by over 30%. Mandatory vacation time resulted in a 33% reduction in fraud costs and a 40% reduction in fraud duration.[15]

At the end of the day we will never defeat human nature, but recommending basic measures can go a long way for your clients and keep relationships strong. In the next chapter, we will discuss firm-specific measures to lower your liability before and after the discovery of fraud.

Chapter 16

Protecting Your Firm Against Fraud Claims

"Fraus est celare fraudem." (It is fraud to conceal fraud)
—Legal Maxim

E ven with a strong client–accountant relationship, it's not un-common for business owners to resist implementing anti-fraud measures. When a client rejects basic advice or imple-ments it late, this may be grounds to consider disengaging from a client.[1] We understand that this isn't always feasible, given the challenges of attracting and maintaining clients.

Be prepared to hear the following statements from clients or potential clients when you suggest anti-fraud measures:

- a "family and friends culture" in their business that would prevent fraud

- a lack of any fraud discovered in the past, leading to a confirmation bias in their own sense of security

- perceived lack of resources to implement anti-fraud measures (time and money are common reasons)

- actual family members or close friends who are responsible for receiving, accounting for, and disbursing funds[2]

- lack of comfort dealing with basic accounting principles

95

- an irrational, but steadfast, belief in the "impossibility" of fraud in their company

Beyond advising your clients on anti-fraud measures, it's imperative for you to consider ways to protect your firm from our increasingly litigious society. More than once, we've seen even the strongest client–accountant relationships go sour when fraud is uncovered. We've had a client sued when she *uncovered* a major fraud within a local government during an audit. The reason she was sued? The plaintiff alleged that the CPA firm should have uncovered fraud *earlier,* despite fraud not being mentioned as a scope of service in their engagement letter! Never assume that clients will act rationally or in respect to previous relationships.

Consider that your client may have a crime policy.[3] While this can help pay for their losses incurred due to discovered fraud, you may be open to a claim from the crime insurer. Like all companies, insurance companies do not like paying out large sums of money. Your client's insurer can attempt legal action against your firm. Their objective is to recover losses incurred due to your late or non-discovery of fraud.

Do not expect reasonable interpretations of AICPA[4] and PCAOB[5] standards to save you from a claim. There are two main factors working decidedly against you. First, you are expected to be an impartial watchdog, the "gatekeeper of corporate governance." Second, there is poor public knowledge of your professional requirements and expertise as it relates to your defined engagement.[6] We would add support for an anecdotal third: for a layperson on a jury, your insurance policy provides you with deep pockets.

The below list is compiled to assist you with reducing your firm's exposure to fraud:

Keep written documentation of your anti-fraud and internal controls advice rendered to clients. Given the low cost of electronic storage and its immeasurable usefulness in a future claim situation, this should be implemented immediately. Any impromptu phone conversations should warrant a follow-up email to reiterate important fraud topics covered. If it isn't documented, it never happened.

If you are already sending regular newsletters to your clients, consider an additional piece on fraud prevention measures. Once again, see this as future evidence in a claim.

Strongly consider background, credit, and reference checks of new clients, or existing clients that need to be reviewed. Confer with appropriate legal counsel to ensure compliance with all state and federal laws.

Conduct regular ethics training with your employees. Seek to elevate your firm's standards.

Motivate clients to consider implementing an anonymous fraud reporting hotline. These hotlines can significantly reduce the exposure for your firm and send a strong message to your staff.

Implement an enhanced fraud clause in your engagement letters. This ultimately serves three purposes. First, these clauses communicate that fraud discovery is not within the scope of engagement. Second, it offers forensics as an optional service. Third, it is another opportunity to discuss the additional services and the importance of internal controls and oversight.

Basic specimen clause. "Should you desire us to perform special procedures specifically designed to help uncover fraudulent actions, we would be pleased to provide such services as a separate engagement."[7]

Advanced specimen clause. "Our services are not designed to detect and cannot be relied upon to detect fraud or embezzlement of money or other assets by your employees or anyone else. Bank reconciliation services, even if provided by us, are done simply to reconcile bank and book cash balances and are not fraud or embezzlement detection services. Additional services that are designed to reduce, but not eliminate, the risk of fraud or embezzlement can be provided by us at additional cost. If you are interested in discussing these additional services, please let us know."[8]

With these clauses, consider adding a forensic or internal controls engagement accept-or-decline option. It is important to document the client's decision. Your insurer should be able to provide advice as to the specific wording for your service offerings. Much like the end of the previous chapter, remember that you will never eliminate the possibility of fraud; you can only minimize the chances and lessen its impact.[9]

Chapter 17

Loss Prevention Strategies

"All I ask is the chance to prove that money can't make me happy."
—Spike Milligan

The below is a list of several top loss prevention strategies. While this is by no means a list that will prevent *all* losses, it is a good starting point to help protect your practice. When in doubt, always work with an experienced broker, a knowledgeable insurer, and a legal professional.

Use mediation clauses for general disputes

Consider using alternative dispute resolutions (ADR) clauses in your engagement letters. The differences between arbitration and mediation are many, and each has it owns place within various types of engagements. Generally, courts have strongly enforced ADR provisions within engagement letters as part of a binding contract.[1]

We recommend that all of our clients consider using mediation clauses in their engagement letters as a way to reasonably resolve general disputes, for the following reasons:

- Economics: With the excessive costs of litigation, it's generally less expensive to bring a general matter to mediation.[2] For a general dispute, a mediator rarely needs to have a deep understanding of technical issues, which allows for a timely resolution.[3]

- Expediency: Bringing a dispute to litigation is not only expensive but also time consuming. Coming to an agreement via mediation is often faster than jumping through all the legal hoops. Getting back to business faster can keep both parties happier.[4]

- Preservation and Termination: You have fought long and hard for the reputation of your firm. Going round for round with a client is both mentally exhausting and potentially damaging. In mediation, there are no winners or losers, per se. With the connectedness of society, a smoother, more amicable outcome is emotionally better for both parties. Whether you decide to preserve or terminate your relationship, it limits the "bad blood" factor.[5]

- Control: Taking a general dispute to mediation will allow you to have greater control over the outcome, especially when compared to the unpredictable odds in a courtroom. As an expert in your field, you can still control the fine details of your case, while avoiding any potential ethics infractions or the setting of a poor precedence within your field.[6]

- Non-binding: If the other party is refusing to act rationally, mediation is generally non-binding and only advisory in nature.[7] You maintain the right to consider litigation, or other avenues.

- Success Rate: Although the statistics vary by industry and region, mediation has an approximately 83% success rate.[8] When compared to the fickle nature of a jury trial, this can be a very enticing option.

Use arbitration for fee disputes

Arbitration is a viable alternative in situations where you want another person to decide the outcome of a dispute. Fee disputes lend themselves to using a decision-maker who has a background specific to these issues and who can issue a binding decision. Even the IRS formally recognizes the arbitration process to settle their disputes with taxpayers.[9] The below are more specific reasons arbitration is considered beneficial for these matters:

- Control of the process: Because arbitration is a result of a contract, you can agree to the "design" of the process to accommodate your respective needs.[10] Within your engagement letter you can stipulate arbitration provisions. For instance, you may wish to allow for an appeal within the arbitration process. The American Arbitration Association allows for this language and process within their optional appellate arbitration rules.[11]

- Expense: Once again, the cost of this process is typically far lower, both monetarily and emotionally, for a firm.[12]

- Expediency: Much like mediation, the process can be faster than litigation. For claims of less than $75,000, there is an Expedited Procedures Option to further limit your time commitment.[13]

- Confidentiality: In many states, most court cases, regardless of outcome, are subject to public record.[14] On the other hand, arbitration is generally kept confidential.[15] Keeping your conflict confidential can preserve the reputations of both parties.

- Arbitrator Selection: This is one of the primary benefits for a CPA, given the highly technical nature of your profession. Unlike a jury, you can agree to an arbitrator who has a background more closely related to your field of expertise, and who has current availability and is cost effective.[16] In many cases, it may be impossible to find a judge or jury with similar qualifications.

- Finality: Under the Federal Arbitration Act[17] and many state arbitration statutes,[18] appeals to a decision reached at arbitration can be prohibitively lengthy and difficult to prove, if not outright forbidden. This finality should allow you to recoup fees quickly without threat of an extended and costly appeals process. Furthermore, the U.S. Supreme Court has demonstrated that it is set on enforcing arbitration agreements.[19]

Continually look for conflicts of interest

Much as your driving instructors urged you to be a "defensive driver," you should always be on the lookout for a conflict of interest. The AICPA requires you to take reasonable steps to ensure no conflicts are present when performing professional services.[20] Further the PCAOB,[21] AICPA,[22] and others all have their particular requirements to maintain independence and integrity.

Increases in firm size, geographically separated offices, and new hires all warrant additional training on conflicts of interest. This search can take many forms, but the below are some common conflicts of interest to be wary of, as found in various places within the AICPA Professional Code of Conduct:[23]

- Providing professional services to family member or relatives

- Providing services to two parties already engaged in a transaction

- Investments made by employees, family members of employees, partners, or their family members in a business to which you have provided services

- Having a client who represents an overly large percentage of your gross revenues

- Any service which justifies the paying of commissions to employees or partners

- Continuing to provide services to a couple that has since divorced

- Providing consultation advice for clients to use separate services in which you own a stake, without disclosing your ownership interest.

If for any reason you, your firm, or any employees are accused of an ethics violation for a conflict of interest, you should notify your professional liability insurance company immediately. Within your policy there should be mention of coverage for regulatory proceedings or disciplinary hearings. Though such issues are not necessarily considered a claim or potential claim, you likely have a sublimit in your policy to help with associated costs.

Client screening

All too often we see firms, in an effort to raise revenues, ignore the warning signs of potential problem clients. We wholeheartedly understand the bottom line, but it is simply in your best long-term interest to screen current and potential clients.

Sarbanes-Oxley has only further heightened the necessity for firms to screen clients. To quote former SEC Chief Accountant Donald Nicolaisen:[24]

> "OCA [Office of the Chief Accountant] encourages firms to approach client acceptance and retention with selectivity, retaining those companies as audit clients that are consistent with their ethical expectations. Senior management at the firm sets the standards and values of their respective organizations ….The director of the Enforcement Division has made it clear that **the SEC considers individuals as well as firms accountable**."

Simply put, if your firm fails to properly screen a client, your firm and partners can face additional scrutiny and exposure.

Before you potentially put your firm at risk, conduct an assessment of your potential client.[25] Warning items for prospective business clients could include high turnover rate of upper management, tight and highly pressured deadlines, a history of adverse regulatory actions, a history of litigation as both defendant and plaintiff, and a reluctance to provide references.[26]

In terms of individual clients, one who is excessively leveraged, has a history of litigation, has a history of failed businesses, or has credit issues, should all be warning signs. Also, consider a client's reputation, their own internal controls, and the level of expertise you can offer the client.[27] Often, an internet search would have revealed these problems long before they became a potential headache. A simple phone call to their previous accountant, as agreed to by the potential client, can avoid many pitfalls.

When in doubt, you can always use a background check service such as Scherzer,[28] Instant Checkmate,[29] or Intelius,[30] though there are many available at various prices. Some insurers may have a specific vendor they recommend at discounted prices, as well as client information checklists and forms. As always, ensure your screening process is compliant with state and federal laws.

Ongoing client evaluations and disengagements

It's worth keeping a running tally of problem clients throughout the year. At a pre-selected interval, it's worth reviewing this list to determine if you want to continue your relationship. While every client will have special needs, we would bet that you have five off the top of your head that you wouldn't mind disengaging.

Beyond being a simple interruption to business operations, we've seen a trend of warning signs that often lead to potential claims or claims. Here's a list of a few warning signs that should start you down the road of considering a disengagement:

- **Client exhibits unethical or illegal behavior**

  If your client exhibits <u>any</u> questionable behavior, you should seriously consider disengagement. This is often seen with clients who make misrepresentations to business partners and other organizations, or have questionable financial practices. All too often this is a warning side for potential fraud within an organization. Life is too short to deal with unethical people.

- **The client is generally uncooperative**

  We all have clients that fail to return paperwork on time, provide inaccurate or impartial information, or never return a phone call. Other common obnoxious behaviors can include lack of respect for your staff, making unreasonable demands, excessive complaints, or threats of litigation.

  These types of clients set the stage for IRS notices, late filings, interpersonal conflicts, and impact the expected flow of work in your firm. Some issues, such as poor internal accounting skills, can be solved by bringing in your firm to conduct training. Other issues, such as a lack of respect for your staff, business procedures, and personal time may be unsolvable.

- **The client has organizational difficulties**

  This can include a client that is experiencing deepening insolvency or continual conflicts with other business owners. While at face value these are not necessarily your immediate problem, they can create undue stress on your firm. Additionally, newly insolvent firms may have additional shareholders that will want to scrutinize or critique your work. Also, playing referee between two battling business owners is a hazard.

- **Does not pay for services or is consistently late with payments**

  This is the bane of every CPA across the nation. We doubt there is a single firm in the country that doesn't have a client which refuses or is otherwise unable to pay. Working with a knowledgeable insurer and legal counsel, you can include payment plans, ADR clauses, stop-work provisions, and numerous other solutions into your engagement letters to help control the issues.

- **You have a change in your firm's partners or staff**

  Over the next 5–15 years, CPA firm owners in the baby-boomer demographic will be retiring. With that retirement, they will take industry-specific knowledge with them that others in your firm may not possess. Additionally, retirement succession planning is becoming ever more important and underutilized.[31]

As new CPAs enter the ranks, they may also be interested in other fields of specialization. Continuing services in fields that lack the requisite knowledge base is tantamount to volunteering for a claim. Though you may be losing clients in one area, you may be setting up your practice to excel in an entirely new field.

If you decide to make the leap and disengage from a client, it's worth confirming that your disengagement letters are current and contain appropriate language. Given a special circumstance, an experienced insurer should be able to assist you in a review of your letter or a one-off draft, if need be.

Once you have disengaged from a client, your headaches aren't over yet. Undoubtedly, requests will come in to release those client records to a third party, likely another CPA.[32] Your insurer should be able to provide advice on navigating IRC Sections such as 6103(c)[33] and 7216,[34] as well as other accountancy regulations, to avoid any unnecessary penalties.

It's understandable that you wouldn't want to lose a paying client. That said, the resultant claim expenses, not to mention the headache, should always give you pause to consider disengaging. Additionally, finding qualified accounting staff is becoming increasingly difficult, and problem clients can contribute to staff turnover.[35]

Document retention and destruction

Document retention was once a key challenge for CPAs, since only paper files could be stored. Invariably this led to overflowing filing cabinets. Now that digital backups are relatively easy to obtain, the paper grind should be a thing of the past. If you do decide to go the paperless route, make sure that you keep redundant backups (i.e. two copies of the same material, held at two secure and different locations). Follow high-frequency backup protocols to avoid hardship should your system go down. For many, this means an hourly to weekly back up for off-site storage. Some cloud-based options may also provide this redundancy in storage for you. Securing your records becomes especially important should there be a claim. Missing a key piece of paperwork could very well be the difference between winning and losing a claim, and potentially violating local, state, or federal law.

As a matter of general reference, consider your state's specific policies, and AICPA document retention guidance. If you audit public companies, be sure to have a good grasp of Sections 802 and 1102 of the Sarbanes-Oxley Act,[36] as well as certain IRS rules. The PCAOB[37] also has guidelines for document retention. By no means is this a comprehensive list. Make sure that you are well aware of all relevant guidelines.

Some records will need to be kept permanently, while others can be destroyed. Make sure that all of your employees have a written reference[38] and a thorough knowledge of your document retention and destruction policy.

Your professional liability insurer should offer detailed guidance on the subject.

Engagement and disengagement letter review

It's easy to view these letters as another administrative burden. Why oversee more paperwork for routine 1040s when you have an audit deadline looming? Besides gaining a potential reduction in your professional liability premium, having effective engagement and disengagement letters can keep you out of trouble in four broad ways:

- **Liability protection:** It is highly unlikely that a CPA will be totally shielded from a claim with an engagement letter, but it can serve as a great basis for defense or leverage in mediation, arbitration, or in the courtroom.[39] Given a trial situation, those with your fate in their hands will likely have little to no experience in your field of practice.[40] Having a clear and proper engagement letter that outlines the exact services to be rendered and those that will be expressly avoided can give you a clear advantage.

- **Establishing and maintaining a professional relationship:** With any new client it is imperative that you provide a clear and exacting account of what your services *will* be, will *not* be, and how they may be used. All too often clients can become dissatisfied with services simply due to a lack of communication.[41] Remember, you will likely never have a client that fundamentally understands the difference between an audit, review or compilation. Having clear, written expectations on both sides can only help to smooth out your engagement.

- **Establish the rules for payment:** This should generally include new clients and existing clients that may continuously "forget" to pay on time. Consider using cash-on-delivery plans, retainer fees before beginning work, and the inclusion of a stop-work clause to limit your liability and avoid unnecessary work. If you take these precautions, ensure that they are in your engagement letters, and that your clients are well aware of the conditions. Your insurer should be able to provide advice and templates for these options at no additional charge.

- While establishing boundaries for a client, it is also a good time to offer additional services. If, for instance, you are conducting

109

a review, indicate that the purpose of your services is not necessarily to discover fraud. To better transfer the exposure, consider offering forensics as an additional service. Very few, if any, will accept the additional service. Meanwhile, you are better protected, as there is no clear acceptance of your offer. Should your client accept the service, this could be an area of practice for future growth. Of course, you will need to have the expertise to perform the forensics, or a partnership with a firm specializing in that field.

- **Disengaging with grace:** A well-crafted disengagement letter can make your client feel considered and well taken care of. Though they may be annoyed at your termination of services, it's much better to have them annoyed than irate.

If you have a particularly intricate or complex circumstance on your hands, consider speaking with your insurer before you disengage. This can serve the dual purpose of protecting your policy rights should the matter become a claim and having them assist you word your disengagement letter to minimize your future risks.[42]

Employment Practices Liability Insurance

Chapter 18

Employment Practices Liability Insurance Basics

"There are only three measurements that tell you nearly everything you need to know about your organization's overall performance: employee engagement, customer satisfaction, and cash flow."

—Jack Welch

Employment practices liability insurance (EPLI) is used specifically to guard your business against allegations of discrimination, harassment, and other types of wrongful employment-related acts. It's helpful to consider your professional liability insurance as protecting you from exterior threats, while your EPLI protects you from interior threats. These can come from employees who have brought a claim against your firm for allegedly violating their rights as employees.[1]

Coverage typically applies to your directors and officers (not to be confused with a D&O policy), management, and your employees. It protects against claims brought about by employees or those applying for employment. It may also cover you for third-party exposure, such as an employee incident at a separate location.[2]

EPLI typically covers three main areas: sexual harassment and hostile work environment, wrongful discharge, and general discrimination.

113

Additionally, these policies will typically offer coverages such as workplace defamation, invasion of privacy, and deprivation of career opportunities.[3] You may also have a sublimit for immigration claims. These arise out of failures to check immigration statutes and often include wage and hour compensation claims. Be sure to review your policy for these specifics, as well as the definition of wrongful acts.

Sexual harassment shouldn't really need too much explaining, but wrongful discharge and general discrimination typically need a little more detail. Wrongful discharge cases, the most frequent labor claim, can often be related to restructuring, mergers, acquisitions, downsizing, or any time an employee feels unfairly released from employment.[4] General discrimination is an all-encompassing term that covers gender, race, religion, nationality, disability, age, etc.[5]

Do you already have coverage elsewhere?

You probably don't have coverage without an EPLI policy for the risks discussed above. The allegations in most employment practice cases are specifically excluded in your professional liability policy. Some professional liability insurers do, however, offer an employment practices liability defense endorsement option.

Also, your business owner's (BOP) and commercial general liability (CGL) policies typically don't cover this type of incident either.[6] These policies are written on an occurrence basis and require losses to come from an unpredictable or unintended act.[7] Given the nature of EPL lawsuits, they generally occur over a period of time.

Though an act may have been unintentional, ignorance of the law is never a good defense for an employer.[8] The plaintiff will generally carry the ultimate burden of proof, but you will still need to prove justification for the actions of your firm.[9]

If you have a policy endorsement for employment-related claims on your professional liability, D&O,[10] BOP, or CGL, they likely only provide very limited coverage.[11] Be sure to talk with your broker to discuss what coverage, if any, you have available for this exposure.

Two reasons to buy an EPLI policy

The costs and prevalence of claims: When it comes to an actual EPLI claim, each lawsuit is an island unto itself. Be certain to take a critical look at your firm-specific risk factors.

According to the law firm of Murphy Austin Adams Schoenfeld LLP, "The average cost to have a meritless claim dismissed is $10,000 to $15,000. If your company's human resource practices aren't quite up to snuff, you might want to try a quick settlement to make it go away. Expect anywhere from $10,000 to $50,000 or more."[12]

Although most claims are settled out of court, there is always the possibility that you end up in a trial court.[13] Here is a sample of employment practices liability awards from 2007 to 2013, as published by Thomson Reuters in their book, *Employment Practice Liability: Jury Trends and Statistics*.[14]

Liability	Award Mean ($)
Discrimination, Overall	192,138
Retaliation, Overall	147,000
Whistle-blower	276,000
Wrongful Termination	142,200
Employment Cases, Overall	160,000

Statistically, there are cases which will drastically exceed the mean value. Let's drill down further and look at the numbers reported for the retail and services industry, under which financial services falls.[15] The following is a truncated sample distribution of useful compensatory awards and percentage of total awards, also from Thomson Reuters.[16]

Award Range ($)	Percentage (%)
up to 249,999	71
250,000–499,999	12
500,000–749,999	5
750,000–999,999	5
1,000,000–1,999,999	5
2,000,000–4,999,999	3
5,000,000+	1

Figures do not add up to 100% due to truncation and rounding

Keep in mind that these statistics are for single plaintiff cases only.[17] Multiple or class action lawsuits can quickly multiply the costs.[18]

Also know that with many EPLI policies, the cost of defense erodes your available limits. The cost of defense, should you end up in court, can regularly range from $200,000 to $300,000.[19] As such, make sure you consider this when selecting your policy limits.

It should come as no surprise that dips in the economy result in higher instances of EPL-related claims.[20] Unfortunately, it's during an economic downturn that most employers are looking to cut costs. This is prime time for a greater number of terminations, which can result in increased claims from former employees.

Furthermore, certain states are much more litigious than others. Hiscox Insurance has stated that, nationwide, employers had roughly an 11.7% chance of having an employment-related charge filed against their company in 2014. Companies in New Mexico were 66% more likely than average to receive a charge; California was 40%; Washington, D.C. was 65%; and Delaware, 35%.[21]

It's worth remembering that every current, former, or potential employee can sue an employer for any real or imagined slight or threat.[22] The Federal Register even goes so far as to state, "The EEOC must honor any and all complaints – even if they are unsubstantiated."[23] Still further, regardless of the ruling of the EEOC, being pro-employer or pro-employee, employees are given a 90-day right-to-sue letter.[24] If your firm does get sued, even under a frivolous or falsified claim, you will still be required to justify your actions.

In the 1990s, Congress updated existing labor laws with a number of changes that have inadvertently led to a steep rise in claims:

- Congress took existing laws and changed the venue of the courts to an actual courtroom with a jury. This displaced more conservative federal judges with judgements made by the common workforce employees.[25]

- Punitive damages were added in addition to the already standing reimbursement of lost wages. The additional potential revenue has undoubtedly attracted both plaintiffs and attorneys.[26]

- In certain instances, the plaintiff's attorney fees were added into the cost of both lost wages and punitive damages.[27]

Additional resources: With an experienced insurer, you will have access to a bevy of HR resources and assistance at your disposal.[28] This is not only useful for smaller firms. We've seen larger firms with in-house HR personnel use these services as a secondary resource to validate existing practices or to motivate changes to company policies.

Look for the following resources to be provided free of charge:

- **Unlimited telephone and email consulting services.** We suggest you preemptively call the number at least once to determine the style and promptness of service. This is a great resource to speak with a professional HR consultant in a pinch.

- **Online resources to include**: An HR policy library, HR forms and administration, law library, and quick guides or checklists to common HR events such as firings or disciplinary actions.[29] Also of note would be employment applications providing consent to urinalysis and background checks.[30] You would be surprised how often this would have kept firms out of trouble and how infrequently they are used.

- **Employee handbooks that can be tailored to your business.** This will help prevent some problems in the workplace before they even arise and provide your firm additional protection when an issue does occur.[31] Also, ask how often they will review your handbooks to keep up to date with the latest HR rulings and laws.

- **Educational opportunities** on HR topics to help train both management and staff. Once again, this is a great loss prevention measure.

- **HR flash updates**, typically via email, to keep abreast of any large changes to law or procedures that you might otherwise unknowingly miss.

Chapter 19

Employment Practices Policy Specifics

*"The factory of the future will have only two employees: a man
and a dog. The man will be there to feed the dog. The dog will be
there to keep the man from touching the equipment."*
—Warren Bennis

To assist you in selecting an EPLI policy, we recommend that you look for the following minimum features. If you need additional help, it never hurts to have a legal expert and a knowledgeable broker look over policy specifics with you.

Policy limits: Work with your broker to determine which policy limits, both single and aggregate, might be most appropriate for your firm. Keep in mind both the average cost of defense and settlement,[1] as well as the large possible cost associated with class action claims.[2]

Policy deductible: Weigh your appetite for risk and your firm's specific profile.[3] Having an excessively high deductible per claim for a reduced premium could be an issue if you have multiple claims.

Your responsibilities in response to a claim or potential claim: Your EPLI policy will most likely be a claims made and reported policy. As such, it is imperative that you understand what your responsibilities are in the event of a claim or potential claim. Just as with your professional liability policy, you must report any claims or potential claims

119

prior to policy expiration, or specified reporting period. In many cases, failure to report a claim or potential claim in the defined time can result in a declination of coverage.

The definition of "Insured": Work with your broker to find a policy with a broad definition of who is an "insured," meaning who is covered under your policy. This should include your firm, the directors and officers, and your employees. Make special note of what constitutes an employee. This should include those who are full-time, part-time, seasonal, temporary, and contractors, if available.[4]

The definition of "Wrongful Employment Practice": It's easy to skip over a definition, but this will help determine what coverage is typically afforded under your policy. We recommend that you look for the following minimum terms and phrases: wrongful termination; sexual harassment; violation of federal, state, local, or common law; employment-related misrepresentation; deprivation of career opportunity; negligent evaluation; failure to adopt adequate employment policies; defamation; libel and slander; and retaliation.

A prior acts exclusion: Ideally, an EPLI policy will have a retroactive date that covers the lifetime of your firm. Having coverage that starts from policy inception will naturally be cheaper but will not cover acts prior to it being bound. This could result in declination of coverage for a future lawsuit if the act started and ended before your policy was bound, or if the problem started before the inception date and continued during your policy period but was not reported prior to binding.[5] Simply put, consider a policy that will offer full prior acts.

A broad definition of "Claim": You will want to pay particular attention to this portion. It should include, at a minimum, demands for monetary damages, as well as administrative, civil, criminal, and regulatory proceedings, arbitrations, mediations, or investigations.

A broad definition of "Loss": Look to see if the definition includes damages, judgements and settlements, costs for defense, pay for lost and future wages, and punitive damages.

The ability to choose counsel: Much like previous discussions on this topic, having a seasoned insurer who is familiar with EPLI related claims is well worth the money. Experienced insurers are typically in a better position to qualify a firm for your defense.[6] This can save you time and money should a claim arise.

A mediation or arbitration clause: There should be a specified benefit in your policy to encourage the use of either arbitration or mediation to resolve a dispute. Using alternative dispute resolution procedures is almost always cheaper and can result in a more predictable outcome when compared to a jury trial.[7]

Mental anguish and emotional distress: Pay careful attention to how and when these conditions will be covered. You may want these definitions to be separate from the bodily injury/property damage (BI/PD) exclusions in your policy. They are very often associated with employment suits. Otherwise, you may end up paying these out-of-pocket.

Federal statutes: Claims made under federal statutes such as ERISA, NLRA, and OSHA are generally excluded.[8] Look for an exception for retaliation or whistle-blower claims made by your employees under these and other similar statutes.[9]

Settlement procedures: Most EPLI policies will give your insurer the right to settle.[10] Some will contain a clause that will allow you to continue a suit but will not pay for any defense expenses or settlements and judgments that exceed the settlement offer.[11] This "hammer clause" comes to light when an insured wants to prove a point by not succumbing to what they perceive as a frivolous lawsuit, while their insurer wants to limit damages. We would almost always recommend that you consider settling the lawsuit and getting back to business.

Third-party coverage: Historically, claims brought by third parties (i.e. clients or vendors) were not covered. However, this is changing, and you should consider strongly the need for third-party claim coverage.[12] Throughout the years, this has become a more popular coverage that is increasingly included in EPLI policies.[13]

Coverage territory: Worldwide coverage may be available, depending on the carrier. Many policies will only cover suits brought in a U.S. or Canadian court or territory, regardless of origin.[14] Work with your broker to determine your special needs.

If in doubt, always consult a trusted broker or legal professional well versed in EPLI claims and policies. Remember, in the eyes of the law, ignorance is no excuse, regardless of business size.

Chapter 20

Employment Practices Policy Exclusions

"Everything is funny as long as it is happening to somebody else"
—Will Rogers

M any firms assume that having an employment practices liability insurance (EPLI) policy will protect them against all claims and potential claims associated with their employees and fellow owners. This is far from the case. Like all other forms of insurance, your EPLI policy will have very specific coverages and exclusions. Below are a set of common exclusions that we often see in these types of policies. As always, read your own policy to determine how and when your policy will respond. Be sure to include your broker and legal counsel in the conversation.

The following areas are generally excluded:

Liability arising from workers' compensation,[1] disability benefits,[2] unemployment compensation law,[3] and similar laws.

This is due to you, as a business, being legally liable for the provisions of these laws elsewhere. Also, you are responsible under various laws to pay into funds which reimburse employees for most claims filed under these laws. Your policy will likely still respond to a claim in which a claimant alleges retaliatory treatment if they are attempting to exercise their rights under these laws.

Liability under Employees Retirement Income Security Act (ERISA) of 1974,[4] Public Law 93-406 (or any similar state or government law),[5] The National Labor Relations Act of 1938,[6] The Worker Adjustment and Retraining Notification (WARN) Act of 1988,[7] The Consolidate Omnibus Budget Reconciliation (COBRA) Act of 1985,[8] The Occupational Safety and Health Act (OSHA)[9].

Claims arising from the Fair Labor Standards Act (FLSA),[10] as well as state or common law wage or hour law, are also generally excluded.[11] This includes laws concerning minimum wages, hours worked, overtime compensation, as well as recordkeeping and reporting related issues. Some policies will include at least limited coverage for hour and wage issues. Additionally, this exclusion also includes actions brought about on the behalf of individuals or agencies seeking wages, fines, taxes, penalties, disgorgement, relief, or compensation. Claims brought about based on the Equal Pay Act[12] or related retaliation are still likely covered.

Essentially, your insurer is stating that you are alone or limited in coverage with respect to properly compensating your employees. This absolves your insurer from being a "piggy-bank" for improper compensation policies. Ultimately, you need to keep up to date with the latest compensation policies. A seasoned insurer can help educate you and your team immeasurably through their training programs.

Bodily injury and property damage claims, regardless of origin. However, you may still have coverage for mental anguish, emotional distress, invasion of privacy, humiliation, libel, slander, or defamation that results from a wrongful act, as defined in your policy.

124

Bodily injury and property damage claims should be covered under your business owner's policy (BOP) or commercial general liability policy (CGL). Additional coverage for those items listed, such as mental anguish and humiliations, must come as a result of covered wrongful act under your policy. For example, you may have coverage if a former employee alleges humiliation in conjunction with a wrongful termination claim. This makes sense, as these additional terms are often associated with an employment practices claim.

Costs of complying with physical modifications or accommodations under the American's with Disabilities Act,[13] or similar laws. This may also include most claims arising from allegations of retaliatory treatment by a claimant under these types of laws.

Know that you may have coverage under certain policies for defense costs associated with these claims, depending on the insurer.[14] This makes sense, as your policy will likely define a claim as a demand for monetary damages, but many ADA claims are often only for changes to accommodations. Furthermore, the fundamental arguments concerning whether or not a claimant is even eligible to claim compensatory damages under the ADA, is a deeply divided issue. There does not appear to be any current consensus on the issue.[15]

Allegations of employment practices violations by any owner, partner, or shareholder against any other insured (this includes employees and other owners, partners, or shareholders).

Put more simply, your partners can't bring a claim against other partners or against an employee. This is a common exclusion found in other policies within this book. Once again, insurers are attempting to avoid collusion amongst the insured's management, or to act as a buffer to in-fighting within an organization.

Allegation of wrongful failure to grant ownership or partnership are likely excluded.

This exclusion is becoming more prominent, as CPA firms are increasingly changing their promotion structures to include non-equity partners.[16] If your policy does not specifically mention this clause, it may still not fall under the definition of wrongful employment acts, or it may fall under the insured vs. insured exclusion. When in doubt, speak with your broker or insurer to determine coverage.

Third-party claims of employment practices, other than discrimination or sexual harassment, are likely excluded.

The purpose of this exclusions is to deny your firm coverage against certain wrongful act accusations committed against your clients, customers, vendors, and suppliers. If you are sending employees out to a client site, this clause should gain your attention. For example, you send an employee out to a client office, and it is alleged that he or she sexually harassed a client's employee. Here, you will likely have coverage. However, this coverage differs by insurers, and some policies are either silent on the issue or explicitly exclude coverage.

Keep in mind that even policies from a single insurer can vary by state. It is imperative that you read and understand your own particular employment practices liability policy. Pay special attention to any additional endorsements or exclusions within your own specific policy. If you are ever in doubt as to coverage under your policy, seek input from a knowledgeable broker or legal counsel familiar with this area.

Chapter 21

EPLI – Now What?

"Oh, you hate your job? Why didn't you say so? There's a support group for that. It's called EVERYBODY, and they meet at the bar."

—Drew Carey

Much like your professional liability insurer, your employment practices liability provider should offer a variety of resources at no charge. The cost of an employment-related issue can not only be costly in a monetary sense, but also create a major distraction in your firm.[1] Each listed consideration should be viewed in the light of compliance with federal, state, and local laws.

Consider the following minimum practices to be a potential hedge against future issues. These employment-related loss prevention measures may help your firm operate more smoothly. While this can seem like another administrative burden, remember that it's easier to keep a stellar employee than to recruit a new one. Proper functioning HR policies may very well be the cornerstone of your long-term strategic competitiveness.[2] The below should be reviewed on a regular basis. Your insurer should have many of these resources.

Employee hiring process and application forms

A proper process of hiring employees can be tedious, but it's worth

127

completing your due diligence. Standard applications can illuminate a number of important facts about a person. This might include employment experience, length of previous employment, reasons for termination or resignation, and references.

Certain issues should be considered with an HR professional and appropriate legal counsel. Some firms may want to utilize a background check,[3] a history of arrest and conviction records,[4] credit checks,[5] and drug screening.[6] Depending on various local, state, and federal laws, these may or may not be allowable as part of your hiring process. While they are undoubtedly useful in a potential employment situation, never be caught on the wrong side of the law. Always seek the advice of an HR professional and appropriate legal counsel.

Employee onboarding process review

Now that you have a new employee, this is a great opportunity to welcome them to the team, fill out any required paperwork, and discuss office standards. This is also a time to get a new employee up to speed on completing various mandatory federal, state, and local documents, benefits information, and other documents specific to your organization. You can also use this as a time to assign a mentor, have them meet with the rest of management, and catch-up your new hire on company policies regarding topics such as sexual harassment or conflict resolution.[7]

Ongoing employee training

It's easy to get wrapped up in the day-to-day tasks of running your firm, but never forget to take the time to properly train your employees. An established EPL insurer can greatly assist you with training topics and strategies. These can range from standard topics such as sexual harassment and gender discrimination, to commonly over-looked issues such as employee hygiene and office romances.[8]

As the world becomes smaller, your employees will invariably come from differing backgrounds. What is deemed acceptable can vary drastically. Use this time and training to set the standard for what is acceptable in your firm. Your insurer should be able to provide general and tailored training topics, presentations, or guidance on loss prevention measures.

Employee handbook review

Your employee handbook is a valuable tool. It can effectively communicate the policies and practices of your firm, as well as your culture, vision, and expectations.[9] They are also useful when dealing with employment-practice-related disputes.[10] Seek out a knowledgeable HR professional, and appropriate legal counsel, to regularly review these documents to ensure compliance with local, state, and federal laws. At a minimum, you should consider including the following issues and policies:[11]

- Employment related: equal employment, background checks, at-will notices, anniversary dates, seniority, immigration law compliance, introductory period, employment classifications, personnel records, employee reference, job vacancies/postings/transfers, and employment of relatives.

- Grievances: general conduct guidelines, sexual and other unlawful harassment, anti-bullying, complaint procedures, and corrective actions.

- Compensation: pay periods, pay adjustments and promotions or

demotions, overtime, performance evaluations, work assign-
ments, mileage reimbursements, and advances and loans.

- Benefits: holidays, vacations, sick leave, family medical leave, temporary disability leave, health insurance, continuation of benefits, military leave, jury service leave, witness leave, bereavement leave, personal leave of absence, and tuition reimbursement, if offered.

- Health, Safety, and Security: smoking, drug and alcohol, safety, workers' compensation, reasonable accommodations, and workplace violence and security.

- Workplace Guidelines: hours of work, off-the-clock work policy, meal periods, rest periods, lactation accommodation, attendance and tardiness, personal appearance, confidentiality and conflict of interest, business gifts, outside activities, reporting irregularities, inspections and searches, electronic assets usage, social media, company and personal phone usage, and personal property.

- Employment Separation: resignations, terminations, and personal possessions and return of company property.

- Miscellaneous: inclement weather, driving safety, automobile accident, and parking.

Do not forget to have your employees sign and acknowledge these policies.

Additional forms and conditions of employment

Certain forms and contracts may not be appropriately placed within your employee documents, but could be part of their employment contract. Examples of this could include non-compete clauses,[12] and agreement to arbitration or mediation.[13] Due to the legal nature of these types of documents, always work with an HR professional and appropriate legal counsel to ensure compliance with local, state, and federal laws.

Employee evaluation forms

There are a number of differing views on how to conduct employee evaluations. Should they be done at the conclusion of all major projects, following the tax season, at the end of the year, or some hybridization of them all?

However you decide to conduct your evaluations, it is always worth having a standardized metric of evaluation and retaining prior evaluations. This can not only assist with developing your employees, but it can serve as documentation of past performances should a dispute or claim later arise.[14]

Employee disciplinary actions

As outlined in your employee handbook, your firm has a certain minimum level of acceptable behavior. Occasionally, there comes a time when corrective action is necessary, but the issues are not yet significant enough to result in termination. Reasons for disciplinary action could range from an employee failing to perform the essential functions of their position, or violations of the rules or policies and standards set forth in your employee handbook.

It is imperative that you have an agreed-upon formal disciplinary notice as documentation and proof of counseling. It also provides a clear notice to the employee on the nature and severity of the problem.

It should also clearly articulate your expectations and guidance on improving the deficiency. You should also define the consequences of a failure to improve or correct the behavior.[15]

Employee termination process review

This is undoubtedly a sensitive subject and an uncomfortable position for managers. Firms should use a termination checklist to guide the conversation, as well as document pre- and post-termination actions taken. This can include a written summary of employee benefits such as severance pay, continuation of insurance benefits, and compensation for vacation and sick time. Additionally, the firm should consider having a final paycheck ready, directions on how to collect personal belongings, how to return company property, and how to leave the premises.[16] While the termination is in progress, consider having the employee's access to your computer systems monitored until departure to avoid any retribution.

As the owner of a business, you are ultimately responsible for the health and well-being of your firm. When you are facing a potential problem, it can be comforting to have access to competent outside advice. Established insurers will have in-house experts to help you deal with these issues, especially those that require immediate assistance.[17] Also, some EPLI providers may incentivize early reporting of potential claims or using mediation to resolve a claim.[18]

When in doubt with any of the matters discussed above, report the issue to your EPL insurer, seek advice from the appropriate legal counsel, and get back to business.

Chapter 22

Employment Practices Risk Reduction Measures

"The best way to appreciate your job is to imagine yourself without one."

—Oscar Wilde

Regardless of which employment practices liability insurance policy you choose, or even if you decide to forgo the policy entirely, consider the following minimum actions to help reduce your employment liability exposure.

- Work with an HR professional to create a properly designed employee handbook which clearly outlines your firm's policies and rules. Ensure that each employee acknowledges receipt and that this is documented in their employee file.

- Determine if your state allows for at-will employment.[1] Ensure that your employees acknowledge agreement to the at-will relationship and that this relationship can only be modified by the owners of your firm.[2]

- Remember that your employee handbook is a resource, not necessarily a contract.[3] Any other agreements between your firm and employees, such as a non-compete, arbitration or mediation

133

agreement, should be executed outside of the employee hand-book.[4]

- If your firm has a confidentiality agreement, work with a professional to ensure that it complies with your particular state's unfair competition and not-to-compete laws.[5] In some states, you are not able to uphold a non-compete agreement.[6] Work with an HR professional or a law firm that is knowledgeable in this particular area.

- Consider a clearly defined alternative avenue for complaints for both harassment and discrimination.[7] Failure to do so could open you up to increased litigation.[8]

- Work with an HR professional and a lawyer well versed in employee classifications. Ensure that your employee classifications clearly and legally delineate between employees who are exempt or non-exempt for additional compensation. Also define persons providing services to your firm as either employees or contractors.[9]

- Work with an HR professional and legal counsel to clearly determine the legality of your vacation and wage policies.[10] Given a lawsuit, your handbook will be examined in depth. You clearly want to be compliant on all levels.

Cyber Insurance

Chapter 23

Four Myths of Cyber Insurance

"There are only two types of companies: those that have been hacked, and those that will be. Even that is merging into one category: those that have been hacked and will be again."
—Former FBI Director Robert Mueller

As the cyber threat continues to escalate, it is imperative that all CPA firms seriously consider carrying cyber liability insurance. Yet despite this escalation, it's common to see in the news that CPA firms aren't taking cyber security seriously enough.[1] From our experience, firms are absolutely serious about their cyber liability, but are inhibited by common misconceptions.

Below are four of the most prevalent myths we've heard when speaking with accountants.

"It won't happen to me"

Many partners simply don't believe that a hacker would ever target their business. While large companies may be making headlines, it's actually small businesses that are taking the brunt of hacks around the world. All told, small businesses account for 60% of all hacks.[2] These sophisticated criminals will then take your client's sensitive information and sell much of it on the internet black market, or *Dark Web*. There are multiple factors which contribute to the attraction cyber criminals have for your business.

- The resources you have to protect yourself are significantly fewer than major firms. They have the resources to hire on-site or remote professional IT services with the sole duty of monitoring their computer systems and preventing an attack. Even if you have taken the steps to hire a company for your cyber security, there are 70,000 new viruses discovered every day.[3] Although countermeasures can be established once a security company detects a virus, someone has to be the unfortunate "winner" of the new virus lottery.

- You're a big, juicy target.[4] Think about all of the personal information that you have on your system: bank account numbers, credit card numbers, social security numbers, routing numbers, home addresses, and birthdays. Your firm likely has all the information a criminal would need to wreak havoc on your client's life and your business. Think about any high-profile clients you may have and the potential impact on them, and the liability and responsibility you have in protecting them.

- One popular technique to get at a well-protected company or client is having *bridge access:* using a less secure system to reach another.[5] This type of attack is what brought down the Office of Personnel Management[6] (where our Top Secret security clearance applications were probably stolen), as well as Lockheed Martin.[7] This could be a client inadvertently sending you malware or you sending malware to a client. If this happens, you could be on the hook.

- It's been estimated that upwards of 30% of home computers have some sort of malware on them.[8] Your employees, as dedicated as they are, are probably taking work home and using their personal systems. Once they email that file back to their work computer and open an infected attachment, your own employees have inadvertently bypassed some, or all, of your security measures.

- Finally, hackers may not be necessarily targeting you, per se. Hackers are often creatures of opportunity, and they use software to scan IP addresses across the web. It doesn't matter what IP address has a flaw in their security; it's now open season.

If you reference the numbers put out by the Ponemon Institute, you'll find you're roughly twice as likely to experience a breach this year than to have a professional liability claim.[9]

"It takes a pro to breach my system"

Exploitation kits are cheap and require relatively little technical knowledge. Trustwave's SpiderLabs provided an excellent piece about how hackers acquire intrusive technology and how much they stand to gain.[10] Like all other elicit activities, a black market has emerged to allow even a novice the ability to destroy your business. All across the Dark Web, you can shop for computer exploit kits as easily as you can cruise through Netflix films. More complex exploits have higher rental prices; you can rent them for varying amounts of time, and they even have sales. Per Trustwave's calculations, it will cost an aspiring junior hacker about $5,900 per month for all the bells and whistles associated with an automated hack-a-thon.[11]

The payout? An estimated $84,000 or more per month.[12] Not bad, considering that the guy holding your business information ransom probably doesn't even fundamentally understand how he did it.

What are the odds of actually catching the person who attacked your business? In 2010, the FBI was proud to announce they had arrested a *total* of only 202 individuals *worldwide* for "criminal intrusions."[13] In short, the odds of catching your hacker are almost zero.

"It costs too much"

As of this moment, the cost of cyber insurance is still surprisingly affordable. Firms can purchase cyber insurance for a premium that is very reasonable, when compared to their professional liability policy. Long before you speak with a broker, we would recommend that you visit a site such as http://www.ibmcostofdatabreach.com/, www.aoncyberdiagnostic.com, or research the Gordon-Loeb Model for "Investing in Information Security."[14] This should help you get an unbiased estimate of the minimum amount of coverage to consider. While these will not be perfect minimum estimates, they are a good starting point.

Many cyber insurers will offer primary limits from $500K to $10M+ in coverage. There are also some professional liability insurers that provide smaller limits via endorsement. In both instances, it is important to be aware of the aggregate limit and various sublimits. There are numerous separate coverage components within cyber coverage limits, which vary by insurer. Failure to thoroughly understand the primary limits *and* the sublimits could leave you with less coverage than you anticipated.

What's the long-term cost of *not* purchasing cyber insurance? According to the U.S. Small Business Administration, two-thirds of small businesses are bankrupt within six months of being hacked.[15]

"With enough security, I can keep them out"

Most firms are looking the wrong way; your own employees may be your weakest link.[16] A study by the Computer Security Institute in conjunction with the FBI discovered that 77% of companies surveyed placed an angry employee as the reason for a major breach of security.[17] Vontu, a division of Symantec, had the following statistics to add:[18]

- Two out of three employees believe that co-workers, not hackers, are the single greatest risk to privacy.

- Nearly half said that it would be more than easy for a worker to remove sensitive data from the company database.

- One in three employees are unaware of their company's policy to protect data.

Furthermore, the Ponemon Institute issued a startling report stating that almost 60% of ex-employees admitted to taking some sort of company data when they left.[19]

Does your company have written instructions that guide your IT department on securing information from employees who have been terminated? With the current speed of data transmission, it is advisable that your HR department pre-notify the computer department *before* the actual termination is to occur. Otherwise, no amount of money spent on your computer defenses will protect you from a threat whose origin was within.

Even if nothing outright malicious occurs from employee theft, fully two-thirds of those who admitted to taking a company's information did so to assist with their new job.[20] Ergo, your competitive advantage can quickly erode.

Joseph Demarest, a former Assistant Director of the FBI's Cyber Division, had this to say: "You're going to be hacked. Have a plan."[21]

———————————

The policy language and associated sublimits within a cyber policy can range from confusing to overwhelming. If you're ever in doubt, seek out a trusted broker and appropriate legal counsel.

Chapter 24

Cyber Insurance Policy Specifics

"Markets are as old as the crossroads. But capitalism, as we know it, is only a few hundred years old, enabled by cooperative arrangements and technologies, such as the joint-stock ownership company, shared liability insurance, and double-entry bookkeeping."

—Howard Rheingold

Many firms agree to the new dangers posed in the cyber realm, but are then overwhelmed by the multitude of coverage options. With the demand for cyber insurance accelerating, it's common for a firm to just accept the first policy offered. This can pose numerous risks if you don't understand how to build optimum coverage. Here are the minimum policy features you should consider:

Policy limits

Be cognizant of the numerous costs associated with a cyber breach. We recommend that you visit one of the cyber calculators found on the internet, such as http://www.ibmcostofdatabreach.com/ or www.aoncyberdiagnostic.com. It will likely only take 10 minutes for you to get an impartial estimate of the cost of a breach to your organization. **Consider using this number as a minimum when looking for a limit.** Policy limits will vary by insurer, but limits of $10M or greater are available depending on the size of your firm and needs.[1]

Retention vs. deductible

It's worth noting that a deductible reduces your overall limits, whereas a retention does not.[2] If you have a $1M limit with a $5K retention, you will still have $1M in limits, after you pay your retention. If that $5K were a deductible, you would have $995K left for your protection. This becomes more important as you select a higher deductible.

Breach notification costs

Given a breach, each state has its own specific rules on notification.[3] There are often state-mandated guidelines regarding notification delivery and the content of the notification. Costs can quickly mount, so ensure that this is covered in your policy.

Credit monitoring costs

Although this may not be mandatory in all states, it is the preferred method to retain client confidence after a breach. It is quickly becoming a societal expectation that you will take care of your clients for at least one year.[4] **Credit monitoring could quickly become one of your largest costs in a breach.** Average retail for a year of credit monitoring can cost your firm anywhere from $10 to $30 per affected person per year, at discounted rates for larger breaches.[5] Retail rates can be much higher.

Computer forensic costs

When a breach or suspected breach occurs, you will need a forensic expert. This expert will assess system penetration and attempt to re-move intrusive programming. This should allow you to more accurately assess the extent of a breach and determine any compro-mise of data. The cost of a forensic examination can range from $200 to $1500 *per hour.*[6] This same coverage should also assist with legal ex-penses associated with the forensic report and its findings.

Regulatory action and compensatory awards

This regulatory action sublimit section should detail the limits for civil or regulatory fines or penalties. Fines can range from $100 to $1M.[7] The section detailing compensatory awards should cover damages to individuals whose personally identifiable information (PII) or confi-dential corporate information was stolen. Take note that the compensatory awards payments may have a co-insurance requirement; an extra percentage that you will have to pay.

Crisis management and public relations costs

This section of a policy should help pay for a public relations team, an independent attorney, or crisis management consultant. The purpose is to attempt to reduce the cost of a cyber breach claim, as well as control or re-establish your business reputation. A recent study stated that 85% of customers would take their business elsewhere after a data breach.[8] You need a professional to attempt to mitigate the damage.

PCI fines and remediation coverage

If even suspected of a data breach, the cost associated with the investigation alone can become quite serious. Your firm can be responsible for fines or penalties that arise from your agreement with the Payment Card Company Rules for violating the PCI Security Standards. Remediation coverage will assist you with a security consultant. The consultant will help demonstrate that your firm has the ability to prevent future breaches to your payment card system. For a small Level 4 merchant, this can cost anywhere between $36,000 to greater than $50,000.[9] Know that this coverage may have low sublimits.

Cyber business interruption

When a hacker penetrates your system, they will oftentimes lock you out of your files. Depending on the length of the lockdown and the time of year, this could have a significant impact on your billable hours. This coverage feature will help you recoup some of the cost. Make sure to take note of the hour retention: the amount of lost time/billable hours you are going to absorb before your policy starts to kick-in.[10] Different insurers have different criteria for paying a loss. Take note of what you will need to provide them as evidence of your downtime.

Hacker damage

It is possible that a hacker will penetrate your system, then damage, corrupt, alter, or steal system contents. This coverage generally covers your website, intranet, network, computer system, data, and programs. The purpose of the coverage is to return your system to its previous state. Depending on the severity of the damage, your costs can vary considerably.

Cyber extortion

This comes into play when your system has been locked down with a crypto-locker style program,[11] and a hacker is demanding a ransom to unlock your files. While we do not encourage firms to pay a ransom, the Assistant Special Agent in Charge of the FBI's Cyber and Counterintelligence Program had this to say: "The ransomware is that good. To be honest, we often advise people just to pay the ransom."[12]

The purpose of this coverage is to allow you to pay off a ransom and get back to business. Make sure you pay special attention to the wording in your policy. Some may require you take specific steps or get permission before paying a ransom. Don't be lulled into a sense of security by simply paying off a hacker; there is a good chance that malware may still be lying dormant in your network. Always have a computer forensic specialist assess your system.

Contractual obligations

We're seeing an ever increasing demand for cyber insurance as a client prerequisite. If this is the case, be aware that certain insurers have conditions that must be met, such as portable device encryption, before issuing a policy. Meeting these conditions could take a good amount of time and capital, so plan accordingly.

Chapter 25

Cyber Insurance Exclusions

*"The Internet is the first thing that humanity has built that
humanity doesn't understand, the largest experiment in anarchy
that we have ever had."*
—Eric Schmidt, Google CEO

While the other types of insurance discussed in this book have long been in the market; cyber insurance is relatively new. Exposures are emerging and continuously changing. If you have a cyber insurance policy, it is worth spending time to read it. Understand what coverages you have and those that you do not. You would not want to find yourself in the midst of a cyber incident and then realize that the method of intrusion or loss is not covered. The below is a list of common exclusions that may be found in cyber policies. It is by no means a complete list of all cyber policy exclusions.

Intentional misconduct

This excludes coverage based on actual or alleged fraudulent, dishonest, criminal, or malicious conduct by an insured. Due to the possibility that a firm member could be associated with a cyber-crime, it is important to pay close attention to this clause. In particular, look for wording that only denies coverage if a firm owner committed the act or ordered the act, rather than any employee or agent of the firm. You need to be covered should an employee be the one who perpetrated the act.

Additionally, there should be some form of final adjudication clause. These clarify after what legal proceedings the insurer will be reimbursed or deny the claim. This protects your firm from having an insurer make rulings on misconduct and denying a claim outside of a separate legal process.

Acts of terrorism

Of course, this sounds ridiculous, as most firms will not be the target of a terrorist organization. But keep in mind that just about every hack could somehow be broadly construed as an act of electronic "terrorism."[1] A terrorism exclusion should include a reference that the act must first be deemed a Certified Act of Terrorism under the Terrorism Risk Insurance Program Reauthorization Act of 2007 (TRIPRA)[2] to be excluded for this reason. Some policies may allow you to specifically include or exclude terrorism related coverage in your cyber policy. Others are silent on the issue.

Bodily injury and property damage

This exclusion makes sense, as these traditional risks should be covered under your business owner's policy (BOP), or your commercial general liability policy (CGL). You should have some element of coverage under "emotional distress," as this can easily be added by a third party claiming disclosure or reputational injury. It is also important that damage, destruction, or loss or use of data is still covered under your cyber policy. Coverage for these electronic materials may not exist in your other policies.

Employment practices liability

These types of claims are covered under an employment practices liability insurance (EPLI) policy, as detailed elsewhere in this book. It is important to determine whether claims arising from an employment-related privacy breach are covered here or elsewhere. It is possible that the personnel information from your firm could also be stolen or improperly used in a breach.

Outside interests

Much like professional liability policies, your cyber policy will likely not respond to claims brought by an entity in which you hold greater than a certain percentage interest, or that you directly or indirectly manage, control, operate, or could otherwise be construed to. This exclusion may have the same impact on another entity that holds a similar interest in your firm.

Funds transfer

This should be of particular importance if you are disbursing any amount of client funds or otherwise have access to their accounts. Under this exclusion, it is likely that losses to your own accounts will not be covered. While a select few insurers are offering coverage for this under a cyber policy, there may be limited coverage under a small sublimit. Some policies will require you to have followed your own internal procedures exactly, or you may be denied coverage. More appropriate coverage may be found with an endorsement to a stand-alone crime policy or specific wire fraud style policy. These types of policies can exist independently of your cyber policy.

Portable electronic devices

Unsurprisingly, a significant number of breaches are the result of laptops or other portable devices being lost or stolen. When this occurs, it can become a field day for a hacker. They may now have unlimited time to devote to combing through your offline files stored on the missing device. If losses related to portable electronic devices are excluded, speak with your broker and insurer about whether it can be afforded. By confirming that your portable devices which store personally identifiable information are encrypted, you may be eligible for coverage. Nonetheless, it's always a good business practice to strongly encrypt your devices, regardless of coverage requirements.

Failure to follow required security practices

This exclusion, though rare, should give you pause. Essentially, an insurer can have grounds to deny coverage if they can establish that you failed to maintain minimum required security measures, such as regularly updating network patches or firewalls.[3] Though much of these protocols can be automated, many firms outsource their security to a third party who is not under their direct supervision. If possible, you should avoid this clause in your policy. It's just too easy for a vendor to miss a patch or for your in-house IT staff to do the same.

Other noteworthy cyber considerations

Though the below are not necessarily exclusions, it is worth contemplating how these issues will impact your policy and decisions:

Insured obligation

In your cyber policy, you likely have a clause which will not permit you to incur expenses or liability without insurer approval. This is important for a number of reasons. You may have access to a number of valuable program resources, such as forensic experts, public relations professionals and IT experts. Should you begin to utilize vendors prematurely or accept responsibility too early without insurer consent, you may be denied coverage. While it is understandably difficult to be patient, especially when your billable hours have gone to zero, please work within the system to preserve your coverage.

Sublimits

Consider the specific sublimits inside your policy. While it may feel nice to see that you have $X million in cyber coverage, make sure that you properly investigate each sublimit. Additionally, work with your broker and appropriate legal counsel to help determine your minimum levels of appropriate coverage for each sublimit. Don't be caught having to pay more out-of-pocket that you initially planned due to insufficient coverage.

Payment of ransom

Ransomware is a popular method hackers use to lock down a system and then demand payment to unlock it.[4] For a firm in the middle of tax season who suddenly finds themselves without computers, paying ransom may seem like an expedient way to remove the problem. You should be fully aware of how and when your insurer will allow you to pay a ransom. Policies differ between insurers, and some may require insurer consent. Others allow you to pay the ransom, but you then need to demonstrate duress. Regardless of your specific notification criteria, understand your reporting requirements, and seek clarification if in doubt.

Know that the above terms may differ depending on each insurer or the policy you are considering. However, the notion behind each term is relatively standard. When in doubt, seek the counsel of a trusted broker and appropriate legal counsel.

Chapter 26

Cyber Incident Road Map

"Honesty pays, but it doesn't seem to pay enough to suit some people."
—Kin Hubbard

Cyber security is a hot topic in today's connected world. Unfortunately, the response to cyber events often becomes more reactive than proactive. This is as a direct result of firms not being adequately prepared. Below are minimum considerations to discuss with your team to plan for what many believe is the inevitable.[1] To give additional gravity to the situation, it has been estimated that from 2015 to 2020, the cost of a cyber policy is going to double, as claims become more expensive and commonplace.[2] Do not be caught without a plan and coverage.

Before we begin, please note that all of the below are *considerations, not rules*. Each firm will need to work with their specific broker, insurer, legal professional, and a range of computer experts well versed in the subjects and circumstances below, *before a breach occurs*.

Before a breach occurs

Every accounting firm should have a well-designed response plan before a breach occurs.[3] As with any crisis, being prepared will help mitigate stress and minimize downtime. During an intrusion, you should be focusing on containment, mitigation, and preservation, of information. This will later help a cyber professional determine the scope and nature of the threat. They can then determine what loss control and remediation measures are necessary going forward.

Consider the following points:

- Who are your critical personnel or vendors when a hack occurs? If you have in-house IT staff, ensure that there is a point person for response, as well as a backup. Clearly define their responsibilities and disseminate your plan throughout your practice.

- Conduct ongoing training with all staff on recognizing a cyber breach and how to implement your breach response plan. While it's seemingly logical to assume that a breach would be seen immediately, the facts are quite to the contrary. Only 2% of malicious breaches and 20% of non-malicious breaches are discovered immediately.[4] Even J.P. Morgan went two months before a breach was detected.[5]

- Work with your IT professionals to determine how to best preserve your data given a breach. Different types of attacks and breaches require different investigations.[6] Whatever your decision, ensure that your IT professionals can adequately explain the procedure to a forensic analyst or other expert.

- Depending on the size and scope of the breach, vendors, customers, and partner companies will need to be notified in due time. Ensure that you have a central repository of their contact information, a CRM that is secure and regularly backed up, preferably not only on your computer system.

- Various organizations, such as state attorney general, FBI,[7] local law enforcement, the Secret Service,[8] and Department of Homeland Security,[9] may need to be notified. This is dependent on the type of attack or breach, as well as state and federal laws. Ensure that this contact information is readily available.

- If you already have a cyber insurance policy, you should become familiar with the specific reporting criteria. All personnel should be aware of the criteria and be prepared to execute the plan immediately. This may help to minimize downtime and maximize your recovery efforts.

- Many cyber policies contain cyber business interruption coverage. This provision is designed to reimburse you for lost billable hours after a certain waiting period. If this is the case, you will need to keep a log that specifies which employees lost what billable hours. Depending on your insurer, they will likely have different reporting criteria. Have a plan in place outside of your computer systems to ensure you maximize your coverage.

- Does your firm conduct continual backups of computer systems? Given a breach, it may be simpler to go back and reload from scratch or recover from the last save. Know that if you go this route, you will likely lose some data. Work with your IT professionals to determine what frequency and depth of backups is appropriate and how you will recover from this loss.[10] Many firms consider weekly backups to be reasonable, but it may fall short of a smooth recovery.

- Does your firm have legal counsel familiar with data breach notification laws for the states you operate in? This can help tremendously in determining what you are required to disclose, who you are required to notify, and how. Notification laws and procedures can vary wildly between states; do not take this lightly.[11] Remember, you may have clients in many states. Compliance with all cyber codes for all states that you operate in can be a major challenge for the unprepared.

- Does your firm regularly engage outside specialists to test the security of your system? Conducting regular threat assessments and penetrations testing can be quite beneficial in preventing possible data breaches and other cyber-crime.[12]

- Do you have pre-selected vendors to deal with a cyber incident? This could include relevant IT professionals to rebuild your system, computer forensics analysts to determine the scope and nature of the breach, credit monitoring providers, a public relations expert, and a call center to field calls from disgruntled clients. Your cyber insurance provider should have a list of pre-approved vendors in your area. This can save you time and money. Consider the relief of not having to scramble to find qualified vendors to deal with your problem in a timely manner.

A sample breach response plans can be found at the following:

- www.experian.com/assets/data-breach/brochures/response-guide.pdf
- https://iapp.org/resources/article/security-breach-response-plan-toolkit/
- http://www.bbb.org/council/data-security-made-simpler/what-to-do-if-customer-data-is-stolen/

Your cyber liability insurer or a quick internet search should yield additional sample breach response plans.

When a breach occurs

When a breach occurs, the steps outlined above will likely need to be acted upon quickly. Consider the following:

- When an incident occurs, you will need to make an immediate assessment regarding the scope and severity.[13] This assessment should help you determine the difference between a malfunction and an outright incident. You will also need to determine what information is impacted and your reporting requirements.

- The assessment should, at a minimum, include the following: define systems and computers that are infected, the possible origin of the breach or attack (if possible), any information that was sent to third-party servers, which users were logged into your system at the time, the architecture of your network, and information on any proprietary or profession-specific software you utilize. This information can greatly assist you when communicating with a computer forensic specialists or other professionals.

- In some instances, you will receive communications from the assailant in the form of threats or payment demands. You may also receive calls or emails with further direction for payment or additional actions.[14] Keep a record of all these communications. A camera phone, recorded calls and a physical log book can greatly assist in documentation.

- Notify the appropriate personnel within your organization, your insurer, as well as law enforcement, if necessary. Your cyber insurer, FBI, Secret Service, and Department of Homeland Security all have resources to assist you. Depending on your state's reporting criteria, you may be required to contact them and potentially your clients at this stage.[15]

- If you are able to determine the origin of the incident, such as in a denial of service attack, you may need to contact the administrator of that network to help you block further problems.[16]

- It may be prudent to make an immediate image of the affected drives. This can be useful to forensic professionals, as well as for use as possible evidence.[17] Additionally, make images of previous backups to help determine the intrusion point and date.

- Keep meticulous records of all the steps you take to respond to the cyber incident. This should, at a minimum, include contact information for those working on the intrusion, time invested, and a description of their work.[18] Also, include notes on which employees were not able to work, and how many billable hours were lost. Historical data, such as last year's billable hours during the same period, can prove valuable for comparative purposes.

- You may also need to carefully consider whether to communicate with an attacker or attempt to pay a ransom without your insurer's consent. Some insurers will permit you to pay a ransom without prior approval. You are, however, then likely obligated to demonstrate duress in order to be reimbursed. Also, there is no honor in a den of thieves, and you may end up only encouraging continued bad behavior on their end against you or others.[19]

General flow of insurance services, given a breach

The following flow of events assumes that you already have cyber insurance. This will vary considerably depending upon the nature and severity of your breach. The protocols for an extortion and requested ransom will be vastly different than the responses necessary for an attack from a sophisticated zero-day breach[20] (a breach due a vulnerability that is not yet commonly known). Always work with your insurer, legal counsel familiar with breaches, knowledgeable IT professionals, along with law enforcement, if appropriate.

Even minor breaches can be very expensive, time consuming, and frustrating. Each step will take time, ranging from minutes to upwards of a year. Some of these line items may be modified or deemed unnecessary, given your particular situation. Unfortunately, you will need to be very patient due to their complexity and the steps involved in addressing them.

1. Incident must be identified.
2. Proper internal breach/attack protocols are enacted.
3. Insurer is notified, either through your broker or directly.
4. Insurer notifies appropriate vendors to analyze your situation and determine the nature and scope of your breach. You may be prompted to directly contact certain vendors.
5. Depending on the forensic analysis, you may now require the following; listed in no particular order:

   - legal counsel to assist with state notification requirements
   - legal counsel to assist in notifying proper state and federal authorities
   - credit monitoring vendor to provide monitoring and education services to affected parties
   - public relations personnel to assist with any public interest and notification
   - call center provider to deal with incoming calls from affected parties
   - additional IT services to strengthen your system from further attacks and reconstruct lost data

- legal counsel to assist with criminal prosecution, if possible and necessary

- legal counsel to respond to any claims that arise from a data loss or breach.

Chapter 27

Cyber Risk Reduction Measures

"Take calculated risks. That is quite different from being rash."
—General George Patton

T he below is a list of loss prevention tips to consider implementing within your firm. Never be lulled into believing that any series of measures will keep you 100% safe. Have a frank discussion with your IT department or contractor about the cost and feasibility of the measures mentioned below.

- Consider utilizing an outside computer security specialist to conduct a risk assessment on your network. We would not recommend using your current security specialists, to prevent a conflict of interest.

- Consider a written plan, given to all employees, that outlines your security measures. Included in this plan should be specific ways you will protect data, the "DOs and DON'Ts" of your network usage, and reporting requirements for potential or alleged breaches.

- Conduct regular staff training on your written policies. Appoint a central point of contact in your firm for security-related matters. Work with your network security team to have a predetermined call-back number for any possible breaches.

While this may seem like common sense training, the IT Policy Compliance Group put 75% of all data losses as resulting from human error.[1]

- Conduct an audit of all mobile electronic devices and erase or encrypt all confidential data.[2]

- Implement encryption and digital certificates for email messages and confidential data.[3]

- Work with your network administrator to have minimum password standards that contain special characters and numbers.[4] Set a digital policy to have your passwords changed at the highest frequency practical. If you would like an interactive view of how secure your password is against a brute force attack visit www.betterbuys.com/estimating-password-cracking-times/

- Take a close look at your physical security measures.[5] It's often easier and cheaper for a hacker to obtain physical access to a server than remote access.

- Have a predetermined Emergency Action Plan in case of a mass breach. This should include call-back numbers, specific points of contact, and specific notification criteria. We recommend you have a vetted script ready before contacting any clients.

- Conduct regular backups of all computer files. Files should be held in redundant storage centers that are geographically separated and physically secure.[6]

Registered Investment Advisor Insurance

Chapter 28

RIA Insurance Basics

"Show business is my life. When I was a kid I sold life insurance, but nobody laughed."

—Don Rickles

ollowing the 2001 and 2008 economic downturns, we saw many CPA firms begin to offer alternative services as a way to generate revenue. Being a trusted financial consultant to their clients, it was only natural to transition into the realm of registered investment advisors (RIAs). Attaching an RIA business to your existing accountants' professional liability policy could actually be riskier and more complicated than you may think.[1]

Given the propensity for CPA firms to have an RIA business, it is not uncommon for insurers to include coverage under your accountants' professional liability policy. However, this may not cover your entire risk, and it does not truly replace a stand-alone RIA policy. There are some very real risks in this area, and having full coverage is essential.

When am I required to start looking for a separate policy?

The below are three common reasons why an accountants' professional liability underwriter may require you to purchase a stand-alone policy.

167

1. Revenues from your RIA practice exceed 20% of your total gross revenue.

2. You have more than $50M in Assets Under Management (AUM).

3. You use alternative investment vehicles such as foreign securities, options and futures, real estate investment trusts, viatical agreements[2], and derivatives. These are likely excluded in your accountants' professional liability policy.[3]

If I'm already covered under an existing policy, why should I fill out another application?

An RIA policy is designed specifically for those additional exposures. A dedicated program with a separate limit of liability may make sense. Claims for RIA practices generally follow the market. When the market does well, clients are happy and pay little attention to their portfolios. Conversely, when markets take a dive, investors are much more critical of their portfolios and professional opinions. Here is a graph which shows an inverse relationship between market performance[4] and arbitration cases filed with FINRA.[5]

Given another market downturn like 2008, you could be facing a myriad of claims. Keep in mind that if your entity is covered under your existing policy, *claims associated with your RIA businesses will lower and possibly exhaust the limits available to your CPA firm.*[6] With claims against CPAs also following the rhythm of the market, you're looking at a double-edged problem.[7]

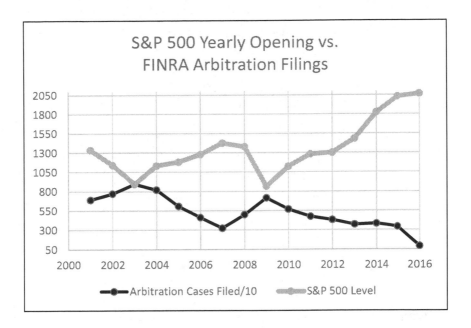

As a general rule of thumb, the cost of defense for these claims will roughly mirror the cost of damages, effectively doubling your overall cost.[8] If you have a $1M professional liability policy, which also includes a coverage endorsement for your RIA, your limits can be quickly eroded.

Another problem with solely trusting your RIA coverage under your CPA policy is that experienced CPA insurers may not have the expertise to deal with more complex RIA cases. It's not that they're deficient; it's just not their primary area of expertise. *You should consider an insurer who has a history insuring RIAs.*[9] They will have the resources, experience, and specialized defense counsel in your area of practice.

Why didn't my existing broker recommend that I split up my insurance policies?

Your current broker may not have access to an RIA professional liability program. If they are a "captive agent," meaning they can only sell for one company, this is most likely the case.[10] When you split your policies, the revenue you report on your CPA professional liability application will no longer include the revenues from your RIA practice. It is also possible that the combined policy premiums may not equal the premium you were paying previously. Small RIAs can expect to pay as little as $1,200–$1,500 for a basic policy.[11]

Finally, they may not understand professional liability for RIAs. By necessity, the applications and policies for RIAs differ greatly from a policy built for CPAs. While this can benefit your practice, you need to work with a broker who is knowledgeable in this area.

Chapter 29

Narrowing Down RIA Insurers

"A father is someone who carries pictures in his wallet where his money used to be."

—Unknown

There are numerous RIA insurers that will offer a policy. But how do you know which company is best suited for your firm? Before you begin to look at policy specifics with your broker, consider narrowing down insurance companies with the following questions.

"Does the insurer have an incident trigger, or a written demand trigger?"

Though this may seem like splitting hairs, having an incident trigger can be superior to having a written demand trigger. Incident triggers will allow you to report an issue, regardless of the how the matter was brought to your attention. Written triggers specify that a policyholder has a written demand from a client, which can be cumbersome and awkward. *Incident triggers tend to increase the speed* at which an experienced insurer sets the tone and formulates a strategy for protecting your business, reputation, and mitigating the severity of a claim.[1]

"Is there a potential claim handling service?"

Having specialized lawyers knowledgeable in your area that can consult on a potential claim is critical. If you have a situation that hasn't yet reached claim status but could easily become one, this option can be a lifesaver.

"Does the insurer have a developed network of specialized law firms?"

Having an insurer with a developed network of law firms is critical. This gives your firm field-specific legal experts who will handle your claim effectively, efficiently, and often at predetermined discount rates. Dealing with a general attorney for your RIA-related issues is not advisable.

Will there be third-party forensic vendors available?"

Experienced RIA insurers will often use third-party vendors to analyze allegations brought by an investor against a policyholder. One particular RIA insurer that we work with has shown that eight out of ten investors either had unnecessarily large withdrawals or a faulty memory.[2] Forensic services can be a valuable resource to help establish beneficial fact patterns and minimize your claim's exposure.

"Does the insurer provide CE opportunities?"

Established RIA insurers will be booked to speak at industry conferences or offer free CPE online, much like certain CPA insurers. This can keep you and your professionals up to speed with the latest in industry trends, standards, and loss prevention measures.

"Does the insurer offer cyber protection?"

For this, you will need to work with a trusted broker. Did your CPA insurer previously offer you a cyber protection endorsement for both your RIA and CPA activities? That coverage may no longer apply if you split off your RIA practice under a separate policy. You won't want to be left with a large gap in protection.

Usually, this is only a factor with smaller firms, as larger firms usually have a separate cyber policy. Either way, you should check who is a named insured and work with an experienced broker to ensure continuity of cyber coverage. If you want to consider a separate cyber policy, we recommend you reference the cyber insurance section in this book.

With the exception of cyber coverage, most of the above should be provided at no additional cost. If not, you should receive a proposal from another company and start comparing with a trusted broker and appropriate legal counsel. In the next section, you will find a list of policy specifics and exclusions when considering optimal coverage.

Chapter 30

RIA Policy Specifics and Exclusions

"We didn't actually overspend our budget. The allocation simply fell short of our expenditure."

—Unknown

Once you have narrowed down an appropriate number of insurers, it's time to start considering what policy specifics and exclusions are appropriate for your firm. As always, work with a trusted broker to help meet your firm's specific requirements. The following questions are a great place to start choosing adequate coverage:

What are your offered policy limits? Are they single or split limits?

This is covered in more detail later, but as a very rough rule, you can take your exposure and double it to cover legal expenses.[1] If you are handling accounts with the possibility of multiple claimants, such as a retirement fund, this can add multiples to your required coverage. Keep in mind that in most RIA professional liability policies, defense expenses erode your overall limits of liability.

What is the definition of a claim?

Far from being "just a lawsuit," broad policies may include written or verbal demands for money or services, criminal proceedings brought

175

against you, formal investigations brought by a regulatory agency, or a request for mediation or arbitration. However, this may apply only to investigations or disciplinary hearings that arise from professional services rendered to a client.

What constitutes claim expenses, and damages or losses?

This can vary considerably between insurers.

- A claim expense is usually legal expenses such as attorney fees, and court or arbitration costs. This does not usually include salary, wages, overhead, benefit expenses, or the benefits of any of your partners or employees.

- Damages or losses refer to the sum of money that you are legally obligated to pay. This is a result of a monetary judgement or settlement arising from your rendering of professional services. Typically not covered would be fines, penalties, taxes, punitive and exemplary damages, or the cost of complying with specific performance and injunctive relief.

As always, check the specific policy language and be familiar with what you're considering. Failure to do so can later result in you paying for losses which you thought were otherwise covered.

Pay close attention to whether or not a policy will pay punitive damages.

Some policies may pay punitive damages, where insurable. Most will outright exclude these damages or be silent on the issue. Some states will explicitly deny an insurer coverage of these costs.[2] Check with your state's governing body, and work with your broker and legal counsel.

What type of coverage is available for disciplinary proceedings?

If available, disciplinary proceedings will be subject to a specific sub-limit. This is often if they are considered as a result of a covered act. This coverage can often range from $10,000 to $25,000. A superior policy will offer full limits of liability, provided the complaint originates from a client and is based upon professional services that you rendered, as defined in your policy.

Does the policy offer you a deductible credit for successful use of mediation?

As we've discussed before, mediation can often be a cheaper option than full legal proceedings.[3] FINRA counted an 85% closure rate of cases mediated with a turnaround time of only 86 days.[4] Remember, these deductions, though not mentioned in all policies, will typically offer a 50% deductible, with a maximum credit between $12,500 and 25,000.

Your policy may have specific conditions as to the type of alternative dispute resolution method you can pick. Other specifics may also be necessary for coverage to apply. Know that if you are unsuccessful with your alternative dispute resolution method, your credit will likely not apply.

Does the policy offer coverage for subpoena costs?

This coverage isn't for a claim situation in which you are a party to a lawsuit or claim. If covered, it should apply when there is a subpoena for the services rendered to a client. Depending on your insurer, they will generally offer a sublimit for legal assistance averaging $15,000. Some insurers will retain counsel at your request, or at the insurer's discretion.

Does the policy offer coverage for execution errors, trade errors, or correction costs?

Your policy may offer coverage when a mistake or alleged mistake was made in a transaction. From an insurer's standpoint, it's understandable that they would offer this coverage. Normally, this error could incur a claim from a client, so it is often just cheaper and faster to cover the difference. You shouldn't think of this as free money. Your policy may exclude coverage or have a sublimit, or it might be subject to full policy limits. Regardless, it will probably be considered a claim and be subject to your deductible.

Know what your policy covers well in advance and plan accordingly. It's worth having adequate funds to cover a trading error well in advance of an incident.

What is the definition of a wrongful act?

Better policies will not need an act to be unintentional to cover a claim. Doing this could limit a basis for a covered claim by depending on how a claimant words their allegation. This is not a position in which you want to find yourself. Look for a policy which, at a minimum, describes a wrongful act as an actual or alleged act, error or omission, or breach of duty or fiduciary duty from rendering, or *the failure to render*, professional services.

Does a policy need a written demand to be considered a claim, or will an oral demand suffice?

This goes back to the incident vs. written demand triggers section mentioned previously. Though there are arguments debating the pros and cons of written vs. oral demands, we recommend that you have both instances covered for reasons mentioned previously. *Any barrier to the reporting of a claim is usually not in your best interest.*

What is the definition of professional services?

Just as important, what are the policy exclusions? The definition of professional services will confirm what is covered. Likewise, the exclusions section will tell you what activities are *not* covered. Don't be caught providing services that are explicitly or implicitly not covered under your policy. Look for a policy that defines professional services as all of your services rendered, and review it again whenever you are contemplating changing your services. When in doubt, speak with your broker or insurer. **This is often the most overlooked policy section by many RIAs.**

How does your policy deal with crime or fraud?

This should be found under the exclusions section of your policy. Most policies will deny coverage if it is determined that you deliberately acted contrary to the law, or were intentionally fraudulent, malicious, or dishonest. Check to see who makes the determination of a wrongdoing. Ideally, you want to avoid having an insurer being the final determinant of wrongdoing, as this is a direct conflict of interest. Some policies require a formal hearing by a legislative entity in a court. Given such a circumstance, the "innocent insured" clause will also come into play, so know who will and will not have coverage.

Is there coverage for consequential losses?

This comes into play when a client alleges that they could have earned a larger profit elsewhere but were swayed by your actions. As you can imagine, if you have an exclusion for this type of matter, *you might pay out-of-pocket for every single client with a baseless claim.* We recommend that you consider avoiding an exclusion of this type.

Are you recommending tangible real estate or do you have a real estate license? Are you working with a real estate agent or mortgage broker?

These types of activities will be heavily scrutinized by a prospective insurer. If you are engaging in these activities or other alternative investments, they will probably be explicitly excluded in your policy.

These questions are good starting points to have an educated discussion with your broker. Know that policy and coverage limits and options will vary by insurer. When in doubt, work with a trusted broker, and seek legal counsel familiar with this area.

Chapter 31

What Minimum Limits Should I Carry?

"A bank is a place that will lend you money if you can prove that you don't need it."

—Bob Hope

Picking a limit of liability is never an easy decision. Your choice of limit adequacy has the potential to literally keep you in business, or force you to turn off the lights. Before you begin to think about a hard number, you should first consider the following minimum questions:

What is the largest single holding you have of a specific security, including stocks, bonds, and funds?

Consider this number for *minimum* limits of liability. Keep in mind that you may have multiple claims that originate from a general market decline, or multiple unassociated instances of alleged wrongful acts.

What is the cost of defense? What is the cost of fines and penalties, or awards?

Looking at data for 2015 on the FINRA website, there were 1,512 disciplinary actions with a total of $191.7M in fines and restitution.[1] With some quick math, we can discern that the average (mean) cost for fines and restitution per case was roughly $127K.

181

The last published analysis of securities arbitration awards available comes from the 2000–2006 Annual Award Survey by the Securities Arbitration Commentator. In this publication, they specifically detail the recovery rates and awards for compensatory claims ranging from $25,001 to $1M;[2] the most likely range of a claim for readers of this book.

What was the average award across all seven years of the study for that range? Only $63,757.[3] That falls roughly between the average for a tax claim and a business valuation claim.[4]

As a rough rule of thumb, defense costs tend to approximate damages,[5] so *be liberal and consider around $250K as the absolute minimum cost of an average case.* Keep in mind that, being an average, this is an approximation, not a rule. Also, if you deal in areas that are high-risk/high-reward, such as SEC work or unregistered investments, the cost of even basic claims can easily add multiples to these numbers.

Depending on your particular scope of business, these averages may rise significantly. Work with your broker and legal professional to determine your exact needs.

Do you have an obligation to carry a minimum amount of insurance?

Check with local, state, and federal regulations. Additionally, many institutional product vendors, and others, are now requiring you to carry certain insurance with minimum amounts.[6] If you have any of these requirements, ensure that you are notifying your broker and insurer.

How risky are your investments?[7]

Consider the following four factors: Is it liquid? Is it transparent? Is it effectively regulated? And is your investment simple or complex?[8] Mutual funds, stocks, bonds, non-leveraged and non-inverse ETF's, and cash tend to be the least risky. Hedge funds, private real estate investment trusts, limited partnerships, real estate, and anything not traded on a public exchange tends to be seen as being higher risk. Expect a higher premium, if they are not outright excluded.

How much insurance can you reasonably afford?

Ultimately, the decision of how much insurance you want, if any, is based on your personal circumstance. Claims tend to be infrequent, but severe, and solid friendships are not a guarantee against litigation.[9] While your broker should provide knowledgeable advice, only you can make this determination.

As a base reference, one major insurer reported that the most frequently purchased limits for RIAs is $1M per claim.[10] RIAs which average greater than $75M in Assets Under Management (AUM) tend to have a minimum of $1M per claim and $2M in aggregate per policy.[11] Once you reach greater than $500M in AUM, consider looking at higher per-claim and aggregate limits. For new advisors starting an RIA firm, minimum premiums usually begin at approximately $1,200 to $1,500 per year.[12]

Chapter 32

RIA Risk Reduction Measures

"Prepare and prevent. Don't repair and repent."

—Unknown

Unlike the section on loss prevention for CPAs, the nuances of each particular investment strategy – as well as local, state, federal, and occasionally international regulations – will dictate your specific loss prevention strategies. When in doubt, *contact a compliance attorney or consultant[1] and think of official documentation with your clients as future evidence when a claim occurs.*

We'll now explore some basic, industry-wide strategies which we recommend that you consider.

Pay close attention to any client who has a very concentrated position.[2] Oftentimes, these positions can result from a client inheriting a particular stock, company stock built up over a number of years, or possibly an irrational attachment to a particular company.

Regardless of your pleas to diversify their holdings, they will often refuse or slyly dismiss your suggestions. Unfortunately, people with an irrational attachment to a stock will often turn to irrational lawsuits when their position declines. Due to the unpredictability of such clients, we first recommend that you strongly consider your relationship. The cost of even a baseless litigation will often be multiples higher than the revenue you're gaining.

If you do wish to remain with such a client, consider these options:

1. *Document every conversation,* including phone conversations. When in doubt, send an email and certified mail.

2. Take your client's entire position and, without charging any management fee, place it in a separate account. Ensure that your client is aware of this and reinforce the fact that you have no responsibility for its management.[3]

Maintain and frequently promulgate effective internal controls. Due to the constantly changing environment in which an RIA operates, you should review your controls frequently with compliance officers, employees, managerial staff, and other certified professionals.

1. Create procedures that your employees "buy into." They should be easy to understand, implement, and ideally come with checklists.

2. Create procedures that are particular to each fund.[4] Make sure that they are not so rigid that they won't detect violations as funds and markets change.

3. Ensure that your internal procedures conform to both regulatory requirements and any shareholder reports, prospectus of funds, and all additional documentation.

4. While no one wants to be labeled a micro-manager, you'd be well-served to have an internal system for consistently auditing compliance to your record keeping and internal procedures.[5]

5. Create a transparent system amongst managers for investigating employees with clearly defined sanctions.

6. Ensure that your compliance personnel have established authority and lines of communication.[6]

7. Have a clearly understood whistle-blower program. It should encourage employees to disclose any potentially illegal or questionable activities.[7] This should be in writing and posted in common locations throughout your firm.

8. Create a mandatory training program of continuous professional education, firm policies, and compliance. No employee, regardless of status within your firm, should be exempt. Clearly documenting training over the year will help to both keep employees informed and can act as a tool for a performance review.[8]

9. Never let a problem go uncorrected. It is imperative that if you discover any deficiency, there is prompt action and supporting documentation. This can help you immensely if there are further investigations or claims from outside entities.

10. Keep a running record of erroneous trades on a spreadsheet. Make it a habit to have at least quarterly meetings to spot negative trends. Alter your internal controls to overcome those trends.

Consider alternative dispute resolution (ADR) in all of your client contracts. The pros and cons of arbitration[9] and mediation have been covered in previous chapters, so we won't belabor the point. Under certain criteria, it is actually mandated by FINRA that you and your client submit to arbitration.[10]

It is worth noting, however, that due to the inherently technical and highly regulated nature of RIA activities, it is generally better to have a body of experts knowledgeable about your profession. Hoping that a lawyer can explain the complexities of your profession to lay-people is commonly a poor strategy.[11]

Finally, discuss your strategies with a knowledgeable broker and your insurer. Be sure your strategies are in compliance with your policy. Also, speak with a legal professional to confirm you are in compliance with all applicable laws.

Chapter 33

Tips on Minimizing Wire Fraud

"In a world of thieves, the only final sin is stupidity."
—Hunter S. Thompson

Throughout the profession, many RIAs have experienced losses that could have been avoided with basic measures. Recently, the SEC fined an RIA firm after a hacker used emails to steal funds from a client.[1] Unfortunately, it's now within your best interest to never uncritically trust clients.[2]

Thoroughly consider the measures below and discuss with your partners if and how they can help protect your practice. While the below list is no means a foolproof way to avoid all fraud, even basic checks can save you a lot of heartache. Remember, it's much easier for a criminal to use psychology, than to implement a complex and highly technical plan.

- Make an established policy to never approve the release of funds without actually speaking with your client over the phone. Consider using a pre-approved phone number. Having a client that is "too busy" to speak with you can also be a red flag to other problems that should warrant your interest.

- Avoid sending pre-filled wiring instructions. If, by circumstance, this is unavoidable, encrypt the email and send it to your client

189

while you are already on the phone. This can help quickly confirm that they are in receipt of your instructions, and there is no ambiguity.[3]

- Use encryption for any personally identifiable information (PII). Failure to do so is not only bad practice, it may have the SEC knocking on your door.[4] Consider this for tablets, company phones, laptops, and any other devices which can store or view this information.

- Give your employees the power to raise a red flag if something doesn't "feel" right. Make sure that they are communicating with clients via phone numbers that are registered and on file with your firm. Be vary wary of sending funds to new accounts in foreign countries and new locations.

- Use multi-step authentication.[5] Consider a series of authentication questions to confirm the identity of your client. Common measures include a PIN number, code-word, and special authentication question. Pay special note to use information that cannot be readily found on a social-media profile.

- Advise your clients to increase their security as well.[6] Complex passwords and two-step authentication to access email and sensitive information are a great start.

Remember that new technology can appear foolproof, but we are in a digital arms race with criminals. The human element will always be the most susceptible to fraud. Pay special heed to reinforcing best practices with your employees and hold them accountable to your policies. Also, describe your security measures to new and existing clients immediately upon implementation. While no one wants to unnecessarily annoy a client, it's much easier to apologize for the inconvenience than to explain why their account is empty.

Excess Policy Insurance

Chapter 34

Excess Insurance Fundamentals

"Vices are sometimes only virtues carried to excess!"
—Charles Dickens

Excess insurance is possibly the most misunderstood form of insurance that a CPA firm can purchase. Excess policies generally provide extra limits of liability should your firm exhaust your primary policy limit.[1] Logically, one would assume that an excess policy is a guaranteed buffer against a catastrophic loss, but there is much more to be considered.

Insurance exists as a method of risk mitigation, transferring risk from the insured to the insurer. You transfer some element of risk to your insurer by nature of having a policy. You pay a premium in return for their assumption of your risk.[2] At some point, your primary insurer is no longer able or willing to accept additional risk. That additional risk will then need to be transferred to another insurer or group of insurers. This is when an excess policy or policies are required.

Your primary insurer is only willing to accept so much risk per insured firm. This is their way of mitigating the potential for losses based on the aggregate risk they accept from their insureds. This is generally due to program limitations, surplus requirements or reinsurance agreements. For accountants' professional liability, the primary limit

193

generally ranges from $100K to $10M per claim and perhaps double the single limit for the aggregate.[3]

Your primary policy, as we've discussed earlier, is your first line of defense when a claim is made.[4] Your primary insurer is the first to respond to a claim. Depending on the nature of your claim, other policies, such as your employment practices, cyber, D&O or other, may respond as well. For the purposes of this section, we will assume that you are considering adding an excess policy to your professional liability policy.

An excess policy provides you a specific additional limit above the limits stated in your primary insurance policy. If you are considering an excess policy, it would most commonly be associated with your professional liability policy. However, excess can also be written for nearly any other policy that you carry. As an example, if you carry a $10M primary limit and a $5M excess limit, a $12M claim would result in your primary insurer paying $10M and the excess insurer paying the balance of $2M.[5] This is, of course, subject to the terms and conditions of both policies.

Excess policies do not normally broaden coverage that you find in your professional liability policy. It is designed to increase the amount of coverage available to pay a loss. These excess policies normally do not come into play until your primary policy limits have been exhausted.[6] They can be broadly classified as being written on a "stand-alone," "straight excess," or "following form" basis, which will be discussed later.[7]

Do not confuse an excess policy with an umbrella policy; they are not synonymous. Umbrella policies are also written to provide additional protection for an insured. They also insure against some risks not covered under the primary policy, while excess policies apply to what is covered under the primary policy.[8] Umbrella policies are most often written with business owner's, commercial general liability, and personal lines insurance.[9] To our knowledge, there is no umbrella policy available for a professional liability policy.

Most excess policies will be written on a surplus lines, also known as non-admitted, basis. This means that the insurance company offering the excess policy is not licensed by the state, but is allowed to do business in the state through a third party such as a managing general agency, wholesale broker or other surplus lines licensed party. Certain excess insurers, such as Lloyds, are considered non-admitted alien insurers, because they are domiciled outside of the United States.[10] Although non-admitted, they are approved to do business in the state, subject to certain conditions.[11]

In theory, surplus lines insurance carriers may not compete directly with licensed insurers. They operate either in fields that are low volume or in non-traditional markets.[12] Professional liability policies are established policies and programs with well-defined exposures. Surplus lines insurers, however, are able to modify their policy to conform to rapidly changing market conditions and requests for coverage.[13] There is less state scrutiny over these policies and underwriting practices.

Most surplus lines carriers are not technically operating in your state. As such, they are not necessarily required to conform to the exacting insurance laws of that state. More specifically, they are not subject to the rating and forms laws of the state that you operate in.[14] Also, they may not be covered under your state's insurance guarantee fund.[15] Due to these differences, you can expect to pay a surplus lines tax in addition to your premium.[16]

Because of these limitations and others we will discuss later, you should always pay particular attention to the wording and provisions of your policy. They may differ from the coverages and responsibilities of your primary policy. Surplus lines excess policies tend to exist in the "Wild West" of insurance, due lower state oversight and a significant amount of competition.

Before you even consider an excess policy, confirm your primary coverages are adequate enough to cover all but the most catastrophic of losses. It should be broad enough to ensure coverage exists to cover the professional services you render. Excess policies should be viewed as an additional reserve in a worst-case scenario. Do not view it as a means to prop up your current coverages or fill in existing gaps in coverage.[17]

Chapter 35

Excess Policy Considerations

"Everything in excess is opposed to nature."

—Hippocrates

Most CPA firms are likely not in need of an excess policy. Primary insurers for professional liability generally offer limits up to $10M per claim, and most claims tend to be resolved for less than $1M.[1] For most firms, reaching $10M in claims would be a serious stretch. For very large firms, excess beyond a $10M limit may be worth considering. Before you decide to purchase an excess policy, consider the following questions:

What are the maximum limits your current primary insurer can offer?

The stalwarts of the industry routinely provide limits up to $10M per claim, with a $10M annual aggregate or more. While it may cost more to carry your entire limit with a single insurer, it can drastically simplify a large claim.[2]

Does your current policy provide the coverages you need?

As discussed previously, excess policies generally cover existing policy provisions in your underlying primary policy.[3] This should further reinforce the need to give considerable attention to your underlying

197

policy provisions. Any gaps in coverage should be addressed with your primary insurer before exploring an excess policy.

What is your scope of business, and who are your clients?

Understand your exposure and speak with a knowledgeable broker to consider whether excess is warranted. Are you auditing financial institutions or providing services to SEC registrants, or are you controlling large amounts of client funds? Do you provide services to high-risk or volatile industries? Certain types of claims can be expensive to both defend and resolve. These factors may warrant higher limits, which can be achieved with an excess policy.

Will an excess policy provide additional protection or simply encourage prolonged litigation?

As with all policies, your primary and excess policy limits are discoverable in a claim. Never underestimate the willingness of a plaintiff scorned to go after every last dollar they believe they are entitled to. Claims tend to resolve inside the limit to avoid bad-faith claims against your insurer.[4] Can you ever carry enough insurance to cover a catastrophic loss brought by your largest client? Unlikely.

How confident are you that your current insurer has the resources to resolve a claim within your existing limits?

Remember that your insurer is obligated to settle claims within your limit of liability, or you may have grounds for a bad-faith claim against them.[5] Well-established insurers who specialize in protecting CPA firms have the experience and resources not only better defend you, but also save you money in the process.[6] If you don't have confidence in your primary insurance company, you need to consider this first, then revisit this section.

198

Are you willing to absorb the extra cost and complexity of integrating an additional insurer?

Later, we will discuss the complexities of including multiple insurers in a claim. Suffice to say, whenever money is involved, everyone will try to protect their interest, regardless of their legal obligation to do so.[7] Keeping it as simple as possible makes it easier for you to move through a claim.

Are you contractually obligated to carry a large limit?

You may have a contractual requirement to carry a limit of liability above what your primary insurer offers. In some instances, these limits are boilerplate inclusions that are not specific to the work being considered. It is common for CPA firms to attempt to negotiate lower limits and avoid the necessity of an excess policy or increases to their primary policy limits. In the end, only you can determine if the engagement is worth the extra cost and complexity.

Will you be willing to carry this level of insurance from here on?

Be wary of increasing your limits, unless it is necessary. In our experience, firms will rarely, if ever, lower their limit of liability. Once you become comfortable carrying a certain limit of insurance, lowering that limit can be psychologically difficult. Always keep in mind that even when you carry an excess limit, no amount of coverage will ever provide 100% security against all types of risk. Insurance is all about decreasing the degree of risk to an acceptable level. Eliminating all risk is impossible if you intend to carry on an active business.

Chapter 36

Types of Excess Policy Forms

"Insurance is the only product that both seller and buyer hope is never actually used."

—Unknown

Much like the other lines of insurance mentioned in this book, excess insurance comes in various forms. Each type of excess policy has its own particular reasons for existence and, therefore, reasons for your consideration. It is important that you fully understand what you are purchasing. When excess policies are triggered, it generally means that there has been a serious claim made with large numbers involved. It's worth seeking a knowledgeable broker and appropriate legal counsel to help navigate the provisions and nuances of the policy you are considering.

The following points focus on excess layers to a professional liability policy. Be aware that excess can be written for many other types of policies, as referenced earlier.[1]

- **Conditional follow-form excess.** This is the most common type of excess you will see and gives greater control to your excess insurer. If there is a conflict between the coverage of your primary policy and your excess policy, the conditional follow-form excess policy will take priority.[2] For instance, your primary professional liability policy provides coverage for SEC audit services but is excluded by your conditional follow form excess. Unfortunately, you will now likely be without excess coverage. This style of policy is much more popular with excess insurance companies, as they are able to maintain a greater degree of control over the extent of their exposure.

- **Follow-form excess.** This type of policy is written to provide the exact same coverage and provisions as your underlying policy, but with a different limit of insurance.[3] Whenever there is a conflict between the provisions of this type of excess and your primary policy, the primary policy's terms and conditions will apply.[4] Understandably, insurance companies tend to shy away from this style of policy in favor of the conditional follow-form excess type policy.

- **Stand-alone excess**. Certain excess insurance policies will contain their own exclusions, definitions, conditions, and insurance agreements without incorporating any of the elements of your underlying insurance policy.[5] Be wary of utilizing a stand-alone excess, as they would need to be tailored exactly to your needs and cover specific services rendered.

Whatever your choice of excess policy, understand that your excess policy insurer may not agree to payment simply because your primary insurer has paid in full. Depending on your policy language, excess insurers are agreeing to follow the *terms* of the policy, not necessarily the *interpretation* of the policy terms.[6]

Chapter 37

Typical Structuring of Excess Policies

"An engineer is someone who is good with figures, but doesn't have the personality to be an accountant."

—Unknown

The method of structuring excess policies is an art form unto itself. The various laws, methodologies, and competing theories of adequate structuring are beyond the scope of this book. The most common form of excess policies for your purposes are organized in a "tower" configuration, as shown below. The below scenario provides a total of $17.5M per claim/annual aggregate in total coverage.

Policy Z: Second-layer excess of $2.5M
Policy X: First-layer excess of $5M
Primary Policy: $10M

Let's consider the following scenarios, assuming there are no issues with coverage between the different excess policies and your primary policy:

1. Your firm experiences a claim totaling $7M. In this case, your primary policy would respond, leaving policies X and Z intact.

2. Your firm experiences a claim totaling $16M. In this case, your primary policy would be responsible for $10M, policy X is responsible for their full $5M, and policy Z is responsible for the final $1M. Note that Policy Z still retains a $1.5M remainder.

3. Your firm experiences a claim totaling $18M, larger than your available coverage. In this case, each insurer pays their total amount, leaving your firm to pay the remaining $500K.

Chapter 38

The Pros and Cons of Excess Insurance

"Actually lowering the cost of insurance would be accomplished
by such things as making it harder for lawyers to win frivolous
lawsuits against insurance companies."
—Thomas Sowell

Excess insurance policies generally come in three forms: stand-alone, conditional follow-form, and true follow-form. Each type of excess policy has its own set of pros and cons. In this chapter, we will be focusing on some of the considerations when dealing with a conditional follow-form professional liability insurance excess policy. This is the most common form used for CPAs, and the most likely to be placed by your firm.

Pros

- Excess policies may actually cost less on a dollar-for-dollar basis than a primary insurance policy.[1] For example, a primary policy with a $5M limit and an additional $5M excess policy limit together, will likely cost less than a full $10M limit from the same primary insurer. The reason is that an excess layer is further away from the primary layer or portion that is most likely to be hit with a claim.[2] Also, competition in the excess market can be particularly keen.

- Excess policies generally are offered in the surplus lines market, also known as the non-admitted market. This means there is far less regulatory scrutiny over your insurer's policy, rates and forms. The upside is that you may be able to specifically design the coverage and negotiate over the price.[3]

- Excess may be available if you have already reached your current insurer's available limits and require a higher aggregate limit. This is a great way to provide that additional protection against a catastrophic loss.[4]

Cons

- Given a claim or potential claim, an excess insurance policy will have specific notification requirements.[5] These requirements may be different than for your primary policy. Failure to properly notify your excess carrier in accordance with your policy provisions can result in a denial of coverage.[6]

- Excess policies will typically come from the surplus lines market. These policies generally do not fall under the state insurance guarantee fund. Depending on your state, there may be additional taxes and fees in addition to the premium.[7]

- Conditional follow-form policies follow the provisions set forth in your primary insurance policy. If you are not covered for a particular claim by your primary insurer, it will likely not be covered by your excess insurer.[8]

- Your primary professional liability policy may have sublimits for specific coverages. Excess policies tend to deal with the exhaustion of your primary limits, not sublimits. For example, your primary policy has a sublimit for misappropriation of client funds set at $100K. If a claim results in a judgement or settlement that exceeds your primary policy's sublimit, your excess policy will likely not pay the difference.

- Any changes to your primary policy, such as adding an additional insured, must be reported to your excess insurer. This might be a new IT or financial services subsidiary. If this is not reported to your excess insurer, there may not be coverage for claims relating to them.

- Excess insurance policies are also discoverable during a claim.[9] Large policies with high liability limits may embolden a plaintiff to prolong a claim or seek excessive damages.[10]

- Given a claim, there will be more parties interested in your defense; this is not always productive. Redundant claims handling and additional coordination can prolong a claim and increase your defense costs.[11] The larger the claim and the more excess insurers you have, the larger this problem may become.

- Excess insurance policies add to complication when determining coverage issues, due to nuances in policy language.[12] Depending on the type of excess policy you have, your excess insurer is bound to follow the terms of your policy. They are not necessarily bound to the interpretation of the terms of your policy as ruled on by your primary insurer.[13] These are areas to review with your broker or legal counsel to minimize the potential for these types of issues.

- Improper drafting of an excess policy, even a typo which incorrectly identifies a primary policyholder, can lead to coverage disputes for your firm.[14]

- Large CPA firms may require multiple excess insurance policies arranged in a "tower" configuration. If there are any provisions in the multiple excess policies that conflict or are ambigious to the other, you now may have additional coverage issues.[15]

- An excess policy may not be available with split limits. If you require additional limits, you'll need to start early on your search. Be sure you are clear on what limit combinations you prefer.

- The duty to reimburse defense costs as stated in most excess policies is not the same as the duty to defend. This means that if you exhaust your primary limits and need to defend another claim, you may have an issue. Your excess policy likely has a clause which allows your excess insurer the *option* of defense, but not the *duty* to defend. Logically, an excess insurer would inject themselves in your defense to limit losses and expenses, but it is probably at their discretion.[16] Frankly, neither we nor any other broker can unequivocally predict what your insurer will decide.

When taken as a whole, it's easy to discern that purchasing an excess policy is not as simple as just having an extra layer of protection. As such, it's imperative that you understand both the advantages and disadvantages associated with an excess policy. With excess policies usually going hand in hand with high-dollar claims, it is critical that you work with a knowledgeable broker and a legal professional.

Directors and Officers Insurance

Chapter 39

D&O Insurance Fundamentals

"I believe that if life gives you lemons, you should make
lemonade ... And try to find somebody whose life has given them
vodka, and have a party."

—Ron White

W e have discussed the likely exclusions in your policy for services rendered while managing, controlling, or operating a separate entity. This includes acting as an employee, director, or officer of a separate business or charitable organization. Professionals with a deep understanding of tax compliance, financial management, and attestation services are in high demand for any board of directors.[1] Post Sarbanes-Oxley Act,[2] the need for financial experts has only increased.[3] Frequently, we see CPAs volunteering to serve on boards of directors as both a means of community involvement and as a way to develop business opportunities. We also see CPAs offer temporary or interim CFO services to organizations.

While these activities can be personally and professionally productive, understand that acting in these capacities is likely not covered by your firm's professional liability policy. When you or any insured on your policy decide to become the member of a board of directors or fill C-Suite functions, you are assuming a personal risk.[4] In most cases, sitting on the board of a public company holds the most risk, but you

211

should always be aware that even private companies[5] and nonprofit board positions carry risk.[6]

Being a member of a board can expose you to a variety of risks. Types of claims which involve the directors and officers can include direct shareholder/investor suits, derivative shareholder/investor suits, employment-related suits, regulatory suits and actions, and fiduciary (ERISA related) suits, amongst others.[7] Common sources of suits include owners, investors, customers, consumer groups, competitors, suppliers, and the government.[8] Unfortunately, D&O claims also tend to increase when the economy and the stock market falls, making them somewhat unpredictable.[9] Your failure to be adequately covered by an appropriate D&O policy could put your hard-earned personal assets at risk.

Directors and Officers insurance has fundamentally been around since the 1930s but has become increasingly popular over the last 30 years.[10] It insures individuals in those roles against many types of claims made against them while they serve on boards of directors or in executive positions.[11] These insurance policies can be used to cover public, private, and not-for-profit organizations.[12] While your professional liability policy covers you for professional services rendered, it's helpful to think of a D&O policy as coverage for management services errors and omissions. D&O policies are a recognized method of reducing personal risk to a professional so that they may lead an organization and minimize the fear of personal loss.

———————

We see many CPAs not consider the necessity of a D&O insurance policy until a lawsuit is threatened or filed. Even boards of directors of well-meaning, nationally recognized non-profits are not exempt from litigation.[13] We recommend that you always have an honest conversation with any board before you decide to join. Determine what liability you will be assuming and what coverage should be carried. Don't feel nervous asking about this coverage; your peers already on the board are overwhelmingly posing the question.[14]

Chapter 40

Four Basic Components of D&O Insurance

*"When I lost my rifle, the Army charged me 85 dollars. That is
why in the Navy the Captain goes down with the ship."*
—Dick Gregory

A recent memo from the U.S. Department of Justice sent to the legal community quickly added gravity to the decision to join corporate boards. The gist of the memo was that the DOJ is instructing federal prosecutors to increase the scrutiny placed upon the investigations of high-level executives, even though they "may be insulated from the day-to-day activity in which the misconduct occurs."[1] Furthermore, "Civil attorneys should consistently focus on individuals, as well as the company, and evaluate whether to bring suit against an individual based on consideration *beyond that individual's ability to pay.*"[2]

Before this memo was released, many companies had reported an increasing number of candidates who were refusing to join their boards due to an increase in exposure.[3] This additional exposure can only further that trend and should add more gravity to your decision to join a board.

With the above in mind, it is absolutely worth your time to conduct your due diligence. Be sure to evaluate the D&O policy of a board that

215

you're considering or are currently a member of. It may be beneficial to have an insurance professional assist you understand the policy. The below are the basic elements that will help you begin to navigate a standard D&O policy:

1. **Side-A** can be thought of as personal asset protection for directors and officers. Under this provision, the insurance company is agreeing to indemnify (pay on behalf of) the director or officer for any legally obligated payments incurred from a wrongful act, as covered in your policy, committed in that capacity.[4] This coverage exists for when a corporation cannot indemnify its directors and officers due to state law or is not financially able.[5] There is usually no retention or deductible, which helps protect directors and officers from using their own resources to pay the cost of a claim against them.[6] Side-A coverage has numerous exclusions, which further limit coverage. Read your policy carefully.

2. **Side-A DIC** (difference in conditions), also known as Stand-Alone Side-A. This broadens Side-A to fill in gaps, remove exclusions, or provide endorsements to enhance the traditional Side-A coverage. This often helps directors and officers with greater protection of personal assets. It also provides greater coverage if a bankruptcy court declares the D&O policy to be included in the bankruptcy estate. Also, if a company refuses to indemnify a director or officer, that person would then have to pay the Side-B retention or deductible before the policy would afford coverage. This can be problematic, as large corporations often carry retentions into the hundreds of thousands of dollars. Due to these two situations, this Side is becoming increasingly popular.[7]

3. **Side-B** can be thought of as corporate reimbursement protection. This type of coverage is generally for a situation where a corporation is able to indemnify its directors and officers. As such, this provision reimburses the company for losses incurred during a claim to protect its directors or officers for an alleged wrongful act.[8] Because insurers will reimburse the company for legal expenses under this type of coverage, this makes the Side-B coverage a balance-sheet protection, of sorts. In most cases, the language and conditions of Side-B would mirror those of Side-A; it's just a matter of who potentially gets reimbursed.[9]

4. **Side-C** covers a corporation for its own liability. Generally speaking, Side-C covers corporate assets for publicly traded organizations with securities related claims brought against them. In many instances, a publicly traded organization will often find both the company and its directors and officers named in a suit.[10] In lawsuits of this magnitude, you will likely need Side-C coverage.

Worth mentioning is that across public, private, and nonprofit companies, 67% carry sides A, B, and C, whereas only 17% carry only sides A and B, and only 6% carry solely side A.[11] Furthermore, nearly nine out of ten polled companies with D&O insurance carry at least one additional excess policy.[12] Most commonly, it is companies that require over $25M[13] in insurance limits that purchase an excess policy.[14] These excess policies are often arranged in either a "tower" or quota-sharing (co-insurance) structure, which will require further investigation on your part. To further complicate issues, it is common to have employment practices liability insurance added on to a D&O policy.[15]

With all of these variables associated with D&O insurance, it can be easy to feel overwhelmed. After all, you don't want to put your personal assets at stake. Don't feel uncomfortable inquiring about the amount and scope of coverage provided before joining a board. According to the latest *Towers Watson Survey* on the subject, 70% of private companies and 80% of public companies had an officer or director inquire about the amount and scope of coverage afforded them. Furthermore, almost half of companies surveyed had recently conducted an independent review of their D&O policy.[16]

—————————————

As a word of caution, these types of policies are quite complicated, and excess policies only add to that complexity. Many D&O policies come with part or all of the previously mentioned sides combined into one extensive policy. Even an experienced broker will expend a fair amount of resources combing through a policy and potential excess layers to understand the specifics. When in doubt, work with an experienced broker and seek legal counsel familiar with these types of policies.

Chapter 41

Nine Questions to Ask Before Joining a Board

"The company accountant is shy and retiring. He's shy a quarter of a million dollars. That's why he's retiring."

—Milton Berle

There are important questions to consider prior to agreeing to serving on a board. While not an all-inclusive list, the below considerations are a great starting point. This can draw attention to some red flags before you take on this particular risk. In addition, it's useful to have a knowledgeable broker and legal counsel familiar with this type of risk to review the organization's policy before you sign on.

"Does the company have a D&O policy?"

Be wary of any organization that does not carry this type of policy. D&O policies have been around nearly 100 years and were created to protect boards and help companies attract the best talent.[1] There is no compelling argument for any organization to not carry D&O insurance, due to the personal liability one would take on. Even the strongest indemnification agreements should not lure you away from demanding an adequate D&O policy.[2]

219

"When was the last time the D&O policy was reviewed by an experienced insurance broker and legal counsel?"

D&O policies should be reviewed at least annually to ensure the latest policy language is used to provide optimal coverage. Due to the highly litigious nature of D&O claims, it is becoming increasingly more common for companies to seek out law firms to assist in this review.[3] Much like tax and audit litigation, the world of D&O is constantly evolving and impacted by rulings from a wide range of jurisdictions.[4] Any change in organizational structure, such as rapid growth, mergers and acquisitions, public or private listing, or financial decline, should warrant a policy review.

"What are the limits of liability, and are they sufficient to protect my personal needs?"

Be sure to note how the policy pays defense costs, settlements, and judgements. In some circumstances, you may be held personally liable for certain damages.[5] Looking at average D&O coverage limits based upon peer group and market cap is one place to start.[6] When in doubt, have the policy reviewed by a legal professional and a knowledgeable broker. It is important to ensure the policy in place provides you with a tolerable level of risk.

"What are the claims and potential claims history of the organization, and have past claims lowered the available limits of liability?"

This can give you a good feel for the overall health of an organization, before you make a final decision. A history of frequent claims or a severely diminished set of limits could be warning signs. As a point of reference, most insurance companies will offer maximum limits to be less than the total asset level of an insured. Underwriters do not want the D&O policy to be a company's largest asset.[7]

"What are the exclusions in the policy?"

A standard set of exclusions would include, "fraud, personal profiting, accounting of profits, and other illegal compensation exclusions, pending and prior litigation, late claims notice, bodily injury and property damage, pollution, and insured versus insured claims."[8] ERISA violation claims are generally excluded, as this type of claim would likely be covered under a fiduciary liability style policy.[9]

While the above would seem logical, given the purpose of a standard D&O policy, a few of the exclusions are slightly more nuanced and need further explanation.

- **Insured versus insured exclusion.** This could be problematic if a major shareholder were to originate a claim against the board. Look for policy language that bars coverage only when "active assistance" from another insured is involved.[10] Another exception could occur if a former director or officer brings a claim against a current director or officer. A "carve back" can allocate a certain amount of time that a former director or officer can be absent before a claim against a current director or officer would be covered.[11]

- Given a bankruptcy situation, an insurer could argue that a claim from a trustee, debtor, or creditor committee against a director or officer cannot be covered. Unfortunately, this is an issue that currently has conflicting legal precedents. Ideally, the D&O policy will have explicit language that states a trustee in a bankruptcy will not fall under the insured versus insured exclusion.[12]

221

- **Fraud/dishonesty exclusion.** This exclusion will bar coverage for any claim made in connection with any director or officer's fraud, dishonesty or otherwise willful violation of the law. This exclusion should likely include a caveat that the intentional act of one insured would not bar coverage for the remaining directors or officers. By limiting the scope of culpability for willfully errant acts, the remaining insured can seek coverage under the policy.[13] This is generally referred to as an "innocent insured" or "severability" clause.

  Take note of the exclusions and definitions section of the policy. Determine if other coverage is in place to cover these exclusions, and ask questions if you're in doubt.

Will your position be a named insured on the policy?

The degree to which this matters will depend on the type of organization and its policy. If possible, it is best to have your position and duties as a specific insured on the policy. This will help to enable coverage under the policy, with the intent of lowering the chance of an adverse coverage interpretation later.

Is the balance sheet of the company strong and stable?

Being a financial professional, you are particularly well-suited to evaluate this question. Joining the board of a company that is on the brink of insolvency is almost like volunteering for a lawsuit. If, for whatever reason, you are thinking about joining the board of a company that is in or nearing insolvency, pay particular attention to Side-A coverage. This is the most likely provision to keep your assets safe or, at least, less exposed.[14]

What are the "notice terms" of the policy?

A notice clause will define who must be made aware of a problem for coverage to be triggered after a claim. Having your chief legal representative or risk manager tied to the notice clause is usually in your best interest. An ambiguous notice clause tied to every employee can later result in a denial of coverage. As such, an insurer could argue that since "somebody" knew of the problem and it wasn't reported, the entity failed to fulfill its obligations under the policy's strict adherence to notification.[15] As an entity gets larger and employee count increases, this clause becomes more important.

Is there a retroactive date on the policy?

Any action that occurred prior to the policy inception date will not be covered unless there is a retroactive date. The main reason to not have an aged retroactive date is that either the account was extremely destressed, or there was a merger or acquisition.[16] Most D&O policies have a prior and pending litigation date or continuity date.[17] These are considered "soft dates," while a retroactive date is a "hard date."

Once you have reviewed these questions and feel comfortable with the responses, it is important to obtain a copy of the policy. Personally read through it. Arrange to have it thoroughly reviewed by both a knowledgeable broker and legal counsel familiar with these types of policies. Never find yourself in a position where your personal assets may be at risk.

Additional Information

Chapter 42

Executive Summary

"An engineer can always write a book, but a poet should never build a bridge."

—Joseph E. Brunsman

The below is a recap of the insurance types we have discussed and basic coverages afforded with most policies. While it was impossible for us to discuss the particulars of each policy in the entire market, you are now armed with the fundamentals. You are prepared to begin an educated discussion with insurers, brokers, and appropriate legal counsel. If you're ever on the fence about whether you need a policy or not, just remember, the yearly cost of many of these policies may be less than the initial consultation with a lawyer after a claim has been made. When in doubt, always err on the side of caution.

Professional liability insurance. Also referred to as errors and omissions (E&O) coverage, it protects you from claims arising from professional services that you rendered. Due to the probability of claims and potential claims in this area, most CPA firms carry this coverage.

Employment practices liability insurance. EPLI covers employers from claims made by current, former, and potential employees who claim the company violated their legal rights as employees. This generally includes harassment or hostile work environment, wrongful discharge, and general discrimination. Depending on your policy, there may also be coverage for third-party claims.

Cyber insurance. This is a comparatively new type of policy that covers you for damages and liabilities inherent in the use of computer systems. Depending on the wording of your policy, you may have both third and first-party coverages. First-party coverage might include notification costs, credit monitoring for your clients, call centers, PR experts, various IT professionals, and legal representation when a breach occurs.

Excess insurance. This type of insurance is used to increase the available limits of liability, assuming the damages are covered under both your primary and excess policies. Generally speaking, you should consider maxing out the available limits offered by an experienced insurer (usually $10M per claim) before you begin looking at excess limit policies. In the grand scheme of things, very few firms will need these types of policies.

Directors and Officers insurance. This type of policy will provide coverage for most negligent acts, statements, or omissions alleged to have been committed by the company or board of directors. In essence, it covers you for the management decisions you make while serving on a board. Certain policies may or may not cover directors and officers for certain types of employment-related issues. The wording and coverages of these policies are immensely lengthy and require a professional for review and consultation. You need to review this coverage if you are considering sitting or currently sit on a board of directors.

Though some of the above policies will occasionally overlap, it's imperative to have a clear mental model of where you or your firm has gaps in coverage. Each type of policy is specifically tailored to handle different types of exposure.

Types of insurance companies. Broadly speaking, there are two types of insurers in the marketplace: stock insurance companies, and mutual insurance companies. Here is what A.M. Best had to say concerning the difference between the two:

> "The structural differences between stock and mutual insurance companies affect business decisions. Stock companies have to answer to owners and policyholders, so if management's investment strategies are carried out with shareholders expectations in mind – seizing opportunities for growth and profit – they may be acting in a way at the expense of policyholders. Mutuals, on the other hand, are owned by the policyholders, so the focus likely will be on affordability [.]"[1]

Chapter 43

Other Common Questions

"I'm a gangster, and gangsters don't ask questions."
—Lil' Wayne

B elow are a set of common questions that we hear from our clients of all sizes. The answers to each question were important enough to be included in this book but are not so lengthy as to require a separate chapter.

Q: What about health insurance, business owner policies (BOP), commercial general liability (CGL), etc.? Why didn't you cover those topics?

A: We don't specialize in those areas. If you're looking for expertise in those fields, we have recommendations for who you can contact.

Q: How much does an agent or broker make?

A: This actually depends on the seniority of the agent/broker, the size of his business, and the individual insurance provider. Typically, it can range anywhere from 5% to 15% of your total premium. Remember, if you're paying a person, he or she should be adding value to your business.

Q: Does using an agent or broker increase my premium?

A: It shouldn't. Experienced brokers understand your business. They should help you better define your exposures and accurately define your business strengths. In many cases this can actually lower your premium and provide tailored loss prevention solutions. Additionally, they can act as the firm's advocate to your insurer and promptly assist you with claims, potential claims, and loss prevention measures. In short, it always helps to have an expert on your side.

Q: Why can't you just tell me exactly how much insurance to buy?

A: No policy will keep your business 100% safe; it's all about probabilities and minimizing risk.

Q: I received a random email describing how my policy is deficient in a number of areas compared to another insurer. Now what?

A: We see this constantly. They're almost always trying to fabricate an urgency where there was none before. After reading this book, you probably know more than 99% of your peers. We'd recommend that you reference Chapter 3, "Four Simple Questions," when talking to your broker. There is a large divide between fear and information as selling strategies.

Q: How do I know that my insurer has the best people to manage my problems and issues?

A: Going back to the "Four Simple Questions" chapter, there is a three to eight-year claims lag. Due to a lack of experience, most new insurers for CPA's professional liability will leave the market within four years. Established professionals with the expertise you want to help solve your problems probably aren't going to entertain the notion of working for a program that may not exist in a few years.

Q: Why do they ask the percentage of revenues from my largest client?

A: When a firm first starts out, it's not uncommon for one client's fees to exceed 20% of your firm's gross revenues. However, as your business matures, insurers want to see that percentage go down. This is so that a client can't have undue influence on the impartial nature of your services.

Q: What if I get sued for $10M or greater?

A: Remember, lawyers can ask for anything they want, but that doesn't mean they'll get it. Technically speaking, this is a psychological method known as anchoring. If I threaten you with a $6M lawsuit but settle out of court for $300K, you're going to assume it's a bargain. Coincidently, this is another reason to have a seasoned insurer. They have seen this method used time and again, and will likely be able to steer you towards a reasonable resolution.

Q: I've been sued, but I did nothing wrong. Shouldn't I just go to court and prove I'm innocent?

A: Never assume that a jury will act logically. They may hold you to an unattainable standard, because you're the expert. The average person has no true grasp on the technicalities of your profession. Due to the technical nature of most claims, it may just be a better business decision to resolve your matter early.

Q: As long as my work is perfect, why would I ever get sued?

A: A claim can occur regardless of the quality of your work, and you have no control over the business decisions of your clients. Prepare for the worst, hope for the best.

Q: How long should I retain documents?

A: According to Ric Rosario, the CEO of CAMICO, 97% of claims occur within seven years of work completion. Consider developing a document retention strategy with at least a ten-year holding period. Check with your insurer and legal counsel for more specifics. They should have a template you can change to fit your needs.

Q: I just started a new firm, and my broker spoke about a step increase. What is that?

A: As your policy is renewed each year, an additional year of prior acts coverage is accrued. Your firm's annual premium will reflect a "step increase" to compensate for this expanding time period and growing exposure. Even if you were an experienced CPA prior to founding your own company, that experience will be reflected in your yearly premium and not in the step increase per se. Each insurer has their own particular duration of yearly step increases and percentages per year. Remember that this increase will occur in conjunction with other normal increases due to higher weighted gross revenues or increased scope of business practices. Don't be surprised if your next premium is higher than what your insurers standard step increase is.

When in doubt, your broker will be able to speak with the underwriter to determine where the increases in your premium are coming from. Each insurer has different policies on the length and percentages for each year of additional work you perform. Know that you can count on your rate roughly doubling over five years, just for the step factor.

Q: A client wants to be named as an additional insured under my policy. Is this possible?

A: This is not possible under any professional liability policy. There is one primary, and one notional, reason for this:

- A third party has no insurable interest under your policy. A professional liability policy protects the policyholder from claims that arise from professional services rendered. A third party falls outside of the intent of a professional liability policy.

- Also, becoming a named insured under your policy would mean that your client would be afforded the same protections under the policy as you, meaning that if either was accused of performing a negligent act, there would be no coverage; insureds can't sue other insureds under the same policy.

Q: Can I increase my limit of liability mid-term for a single engagement?

A: Usually these requests come from potential contracts that require a specific amount of insurance. Typically, these requests come from businesses that are just placing boilerplate language in a contract. If approved, some insurers may require you to increase your overall limit, while others may offer a specific excess limit endorsement. While it is possible for some insurers to increase your limits for specific engagements, insurers are generally hesitant to do this.

Q: Who are the best professional liability insurers in the marketplace?

A: For most CPA firms, you should start your search with the two stalwarts of the industry: CAMICO and CNA.

Q: I have another question that wasn't covered in this book. Can you answer it?

A: Feel free to send an email to Joseph. (joseph@cplbrokers.com). If possible, we will do our best to answer your questions. Also, we will use additional questions to update this book as needed.

Additional Service Requests and Contact Information

CPA firms come to us when they are frustrated with the standard renewal process of "Give me your money, and talk to me next year." They are looking to partner with a specialized broker who can proactively assist their business with solutions to problems and not just collect a premium payment.

For the right clients, we begin by better defining their firm-specific liability exposures. This enables us to partner them with a proactive insurer, significantly enhance their loss prevention knowledge and internal controls throughout their firm, and drastically lower their risk of claims and losses. In short, we train you on your practice insurance so you can get back to focusing on growing or maintaining your firm.

While we can provide dramatic results, we find that slightly less than half of the firms we speak with can benefit from our expertise. But if addressing these problems are important to you, we'd be happy to learn more about your situation to see if we would be the right fit.

Joseph E. Brunsman: joseph@cplbrokers.com

Daniel W. Hudson: dhudson@cplbrokers.com

Notes and References

We spent quite a lot of time researching the various sources in this book. Our hope is that the text of this book will spark an interest in you to utilize these sources for further discovery and clarification.

Chapter 1 Professional Liability Insurance Basics

[1] Rodin, A. J. (2011). Rethinking the Purchase of Malpractice Self-Insurance. *The CPA Journal*. Retrieved January 12, 2016, from http://archives.cpajournal.com/

Can be accessed via either the CPA Journal website, or via http://insurancenewsnet.com/oarticle/Rethinking-the-Purchase-of-Malpractice-Self-Insurance-[CPA-Journal-The]-a-291206

Chapter 2 Warning Signs

[1] Murphy, K. M., Esq. (2016, February 5). Interview with Kevin Murphy [Telephone interview]. Kevin Murphy serves as Carr Maloney's managing attorney and has earned a reputation as an effective advocate and litigator. Kevin concentrates his practice in the areas of commercial litigation, estate and trust disputes, and professional liability defense, especially the defense of accountants, lawyers, architects, brokers and fiduciaries. He has over three decades of experience in trial and appellate courts, and in arbitrations and mediations. In addition, Kevin has represented numerous clients in governmental and congressional investigations. His clients include corporations, corporate fiduciaries, beneficiaries and legatees, financial institutions, accounting firms, law firms, architects, contractors, and developers.

[2] Ryles, T. (2008, October). Disclosing Policy Limits in Liability Claims: A Landmine for Bad Faith. Retrieved October, 2015, from https://www.irmi.com/articles/expert-commentary/disclosing-policy-limits-in-liability-claims-a-landmine-for-bad-faith

[3] Jerry, R. J., & Richmond, D. R. (2012). Insurers' Liability for Bad Faith. In *Understanding Insurance Law* (5th ed., pp. 162–164). New Providence, NJ: LexisNexis.

[4] Bryan, M., & Shapiro, R. I. (2013, October). Managing Professional Liability Litigation Against Accounting Firms (Part 2). Retrieved December, 2015, from http://www.lplegal.com/sites/default/files/CPFM_09_10_13_Shapiro[4].pdf

Originally Published in the CPA Practice Management Forum

[5] Wilck, D. S., & Shah, K. (2010, November 2). Coverage Concerns In Burning Limits Policies. Retrieved November 18, 2015, from http://www.rivkinradler.com/publications/coverage-concerns-in-burning-limits-policies/

[6] Rosario, R. (2015, September). *The Status of CAMICO and the Insurance Industry*. Speech presented at Select Policyholder Luncheon, Bethesda, MD.

[7] Shuster, D. J., Esq., & Motley, K. D. (2015, February). The Right to Independent Counsel of Your Choice in the Defense of a Professional Liability Claim. Retrieved February, 2016, from http://www.kramonandgraham.com/siteFiles/News/DJS Article 02-2015.pdf

[8] Rodin, A. J. (2011). Rethinking the Purchase of Malpractice Self-Insurance. *The CPA Journal*. Retrieved January 12, 2016, from http://archives.cpajournal.com/ Can be accessed via either the CPA Journal website, or via http://insurancenewsnet.com/oarticle/Rethinking-the-Purchase-of-Malpractice-Self-Insurance-[CPA-Journal-The]-a-291206

[9] Definition: Consent to Settlement Clause. (n.d.). Retrieved March, 2016, from https://www.irmi.com/online/insurance-glossary/terms/c/consent-to-settlement-clause.aspx

10 Bryan, M., & Shapiro, R. I. (2013, October). Managing Professional Liability Litigation Against Accounting Firms (Part 2). Retrieved December, 2015, from http://www.lplegal.com/sites/default/files/CPFM_09_10_13_Shapiro[4].pdf Originally Published in the CPA Practice Management Forum

[11] Rodin, A. J. (2011). Rethinking the Purchase of Malpractice Self-Insurance. *The CPA Journal.* Retrieved January 12, 2016, from http://archives.cpajournal.com/

Can be accessed via either the CPA Journal website, or via http://insurancenewsnet.com/oarticle/Rethinking-the-Purchase-of-Malpractice-Self-Insurance-[CPA-Journal-The]-a-291206

[12] Rosario, R. (2015, September). *The Status of CAMICO and the Insurance Industry.* Speech presented at Select Policyholder Luncheon, Bethesda, MD.

[13] American Bar Association Standing Committee on Lawyers' Professional Liability Extended Reporting ("Tail") Coverage. (2013, April). Retrieved December, 2015, from http://www.americanbar.org/content/dam/aba/administrative/lawyers_professional_liability/ls_lpl_tail_coverage_faq_glossary.authcheckdam.pdf

Chapter 3 Four Simple Questions

[1] Malpractice Insurance Guide 2014. (2014, October). Retrieved August, 2015, from http://cdn.accountingtoday.com/pdfs/ACT1014_Malpractice.pdf

[2] Rosario, R. (2015, September). *The Status of CAMICO and the Insurance Industry.* Speech presented at Select Policyholder Luncheon, Bethesda, MD.

[3] Fitzpatrick, Sean M., Fear is the Key: A Behavioral Guide to Underwriting Cycles. Connecticut Insurance Law Journal, Vol. 10, No. 2, pp. 255–75, 2004. Available at SSRN: http://ssrn.com/abstract=690316

Chapter 4 Professional Liability Policy Specifics

[1] Company, A. M. (2014). Important Functions of Insurance Organizations. In *Understanding the Insurance Industry: An Overview for Those Working With and in One of the World's Most Interesting and Vital Industries* (2014 ed., pp. 7–9). AM Best Company.

[2] Rosario, R. (2015, September). *The Status of CAMICO and the Insurance Industry.* Speech presented at Select Policyholder Luncheon, Bethesda, MD.

3 CAMICO Insurance Company. (2011, August). Don't Miss Out on Free CPE. Retrieved October, 2015, from http://camico.com/blog/Dont_Miss_Out_on_Free_CPE

4 CAMICO Insurance Company. (n.d.). CAMICO Resource Center. Retrieved May, 2015, from https://member.camico.com/portal/RESOURCE-CENTERS

5 CAMICO Insurance Company, Accountants Professional Liability Insurance Policy, PL-1000-A (rev. 07/14), Benefits Available to Members of CAMICO Mutual Insurance Company in Addition to the Policy. From http://www.camico.com/sites/default/files/PL-1000-A_Base%20Policy_0714%20%28Specimen%29.pdf

6 CAMICO Insurance for CPAs. (2015, September 22). CAMICO Members-Only Site Tutorial-09222015 [Video File]. Retrieved from https://www.youtube.com/watch?v=arFGmLHKrT8

7 Malpractice Insurance Guide 2014. (2014, October). Retrieved August, 2015, from http://cdn.accountingto-day.com/pdfs/ACT1014_Malpractice.pdf

8 Jerry, R. J., & Richmond, D. R. (2012). Notice of Loss Provisions. In *Understanding Insurance Law* (5th ed., pp. 577–81). New Providence, NJ: LexisNexis.

9 Rodin, A. J. (2011). Rethinking the Purchase of Malpractice Self-Insurance. *The CPA Journal*. Retrieved January 12, 2016, from http://archives.cpajournal.com/

Can be accessed via either the CPA Journal website, or via http://insurancenewsnet.com/oarticle/Rethinking-the-Purchase-of-Malpractice-Self-Insurance-[CPA-Journal-The]-a-291206

10 Wyle, D. (2012, July 27). What Tax Outsourcing Looks Like Today. Retrieved March, 2016, from http://www.cpapracticeadvisor.com/article/10741227/what-tax-outsourcing-looks-like-today

11 Feldscher, J. H. (2003, December 18). Application of the Innocent Insured Clause. Retrieved from http://professionalliabilitymatters.com/2013/12/18/application-of-the-innocent-insured-clause/

12 Travelers Casualty and Surety Company of America. (2014). Fidelity and Crime Coverage for Privately Held Companies. Retrieved April, 2016, from https://www.travelers.com/business-insurance/management-professional-liability/documents/59218.pdf

13 McCullough, Campbell & Lane, LLC. (n.d.). Jurisdictional Analysis (of punitive damages by state). Retrieved February, 2016, from http://www.mcandl.com/puni_states.html

14 Jerry, R. J., & Richmond, D. R. (2012). The Insurer's Duty to Defend. In *Understanding Insurance Law* (5th ed., pp. 792–6). New Providence, NJ: LexisNexis.

15 Shuster, D. J., Esq., & Motley, K. D. (2015, February). The Right to Independent Counsel of Your Choice in the Defense of a Professional Liability Claim. Retrieved February, 2016, from http://www.kramonandgraham.com/siteFiles/News/DJS Article 02-2015.pdf Page 4

16 Rodin, A. J. (2011). Rethinking the Purchase of Malpractice Self-Insurance. *The CPA Journal*. Retrieved January 12, 2016, from http://archives.cpajournal.com/

Can be accessed via either the CPA Journal website, or via http://insurancenewsnet.com/oarticle/Rethinking-the-Purchase-of-Malpractice-Self-Insurance-[CPA-Journal-The]-a-291206

17 Rosario, R. (2015, September). *The Status of CAMICO and the Insurance Industry*. Speech presented at Select Policyholder Luncheon, Bethesda, MD.

18 International Risk Management Institute, Inc. (n.d.). Extended Reporting Period (ERP). Retrieved September, 2015, from http://www.irmi.com/online/insurance-glossary/terms/e/extended-reporting-period-erp.aspx

19 American Bar Association Standing Committee on Lawyers' Professional Liability Extended Reporting ("Tail") Coverage. (2013, April). Retrieved

December, 2015, from http://www.americanbar.org/content/dam/aba/administrative/lawyers_professional_liability/ls_lpl_tail_coverage_faq_glossary.authcheckdam.pdf

[20] U.S. Securities and Exchange Commission. (2011, January). Study on Investment Advisers and Broker-Dealers. Retrieved April, 2016, from http://www.sec.gov/news/studies/2011/913studyfinal.pdf

[21] PricewaterhouseCoopers LLP. (2015, April). Coming Into Focus: 2014 Securities Litigation Study. Retrieved February, 2016, from http://www.pwc.com/us/en/forensic-services/publications/2014-securities-litigation-study.html

[22] National Conference of State Legislatures. (2016, April 1). Security Breach Notification Laws. Retrieved April, 2016, from http://www.ncsl.org/research/telecommunications-and-information-technology/security-breach-notification-laws.aspx

[23] Crain Communications Inc. (2014, July). Insurers struggle to get grip on burgeoning cyber risk market. Retrieved January, 2016, from http://www.businessinsurance.com/article/20140714/NEWS04/140719946

[24] Wells Media Group Inc. (2015, November 4). CAMICO Broadens Protection for Continuously Renewing CPA Policyholders. Retrieved November, 2015, from http://www.insurancejournal.com/news/national/2015/11/04/387414.htm

Chapter 5 Professional Liability Exclusions

[1] Jerry, R. J., & Richmond, D. R. (2012). Trouble Spots In Contract Formation. In *Understanding Insurance Law* (5th ed., pp. 192–3). New Providence, NJ: LexisNexis.

[2] Jerry, R. J., & Richmond, D. R. (2012). Trouble Spots In Contract Formation. In *Understanding Insurance Law* (5th ed., pp. 193–5). New Providence, NJ: LexisNexis.

[3] Jerry, R. J., & Richmond, D. R. (2012). Trouble Spots In Contract Formation. In *Understanding Insurance Law* (5th ed., pp. 195–6). New Providence, NJ: LexisNexis.

[4] Jerry, R. J., & Richmond, D. R. (2012). Scope of Obligations: Persons and Interests Protected. In *Understanding Insurance Law* (5th ed., pp. 303). New Providence, NJ: LexisNexis.

[5] American Institute of Certified Public Accountants, Inc. (2015, October 26). AICPA Code of Professional Conduct. Retrieved December, 2015, from http://www.aicpa.org/Research/Standards/CodeofConduct/DownloadableDocuments/2014December15ContentAsof2015October26Codeof Conduct.pdf

[6]International Risk Management Institute, Inc. (n.d.). Employment practices liability insurance (EPLI). Retrieved February, 2016, from http://www.irmi.com/online/insurance-glossary/terms/e/employment-practices-liability-insurance-epli.aspx

[7] USLaw Inc. (n.d.). Collusion Law & Legal Definition. Retrieved April, 2016, from http://definitions.uslegal.com/c/collusion/

[8] International Risk Management Institute, Inc. (n.d.). Insured versus Insured Exclusion. Retrieved February, 2016, from https://www.irmi.com/online/insurance-glossary/terms/i/insured-versus-insured-exclusion.aspx

[9] Florian, G. M. (2016, February 14). State of Accountants' Professional Liability Industry [Telephone interview].

Vice President of Underwriting and Policy Services at CAMICO Insurance, Gary Florian has more than 30 years of experience in underwriting, business development, product management, and insurance production.

[10] Florian, G. M. (2016, February 14). State of Accountants' Professional Liability Industry [Telephone interview].

[11] USLaw Inc. (n.d.). Business-Risk Exclusion Law & Legal Definition. Retrieved April, 2016, from http://definitions.uslegal.com/b/business--risk-exclusion/

[12] International Risk Management Institute, Inc. (n.d.). Return of professional fees exclusion. Retrieved February, 2016, from https://www.irmi.com/online/insurance-glossary/terms/r/return-of-professional-fees-exclusion.aspx

[13] International Risk Management Institute, Inc. (n.d.). Punitive damages. Retrieved February, 2016, from https://www.irmi.com/online/insurance-glossary/terms/p/punitive-damages.aspx

[14] McCullough, Campbell & Lane, LLC. (n.d.). Insurability of Punitive Damages. Retrieved February, 2016, from http://www.mcandl.com/puni_frame.html

[15] McCullough, Campbell & Lane, LLC. (n.d.). JURISDICTIONAL ANALYSIS (of punitive damages by state). Retrieved February, 2016, from http://www.mcandl.com/puni_states.html

[16] United States Department of Justice, Civil Rights Division. (n.d.). Americans With Disabilities Website. Retrieved January, 2016, from http://www.ada.gov/

[17] Weimer, B. D., Satre, E. D., Whitman, A. F., & Speidel, T. M. (2012). EPL Policy Coverages and Exclusion. In *Employment Practices Liability: Guide to Risk Exposures and Coverage* (pp. 19–22). Erlanger, KY: The National Underwriter Company.

Chapter 6 What Minimum Limits Should I Carry?

[1] Rosario, R. (2015, September). *The Status of CAMICO and the Insurance Industry*. Speech presented at Select Policyholder Luncheon, Bethesda, MD.

[2] CAMICO Insurance Co. (2007, Fall). What's the Right Policy Limit for Your Firm? *IMPACT Magazine*, (77).

[3] Malpractice Insurance Guide 2014. (2014, October). Retrieved August, 2015, from http://cdn.accountingto-day.com/pdfs/ACT1014_Malpractice.pdf

[4] United States, California State Government. (n.d.). *CORPORATIONS CODE SECTION 16951–62*. Retrieved February, 2016, from http://www.leginfo.ca.gov/cgi-bin/displaycode?section=corp&group=16001-17000&file=16951-16962

Example of the CA state requirements for insurance. Check with your own particular state regulations for further clarification.

[5] Will, D., CPA/ABV/CFF, CFE. (2015, November). *Risk Management Best Practices and Current Events*. Lecture presented at CAMICO Policyholder Luncheon, Bethesda, MD.

[6] Dodsworth, J. A. (1997, September). Risk Management and High-Net-Worth Clients. *The CPA Journal*. Retrieved February, 2016, from https://www.questia.com/magazine/1P3-14022944/risk-management-and-high-net-worth-clients

[7] Dodsworth, J. A. (1997, September). Risk Management and High-Net-Worth Clients. *The CPA Journal*. Retrieved February, 2016, from https://www.questia.com/magazine/1P3-14022944/risk-management-and-high-net-worth-clients

[8] Ethridge, J. R., Marsh, T., & Revelt, B. (2007, April). Engagement Risk: Perceptions And Strategies From Audit Partners. *Journal Of Business & Economic Research*, 5(4), 25–32.

[9] Jerry, R. J., & Richmond, D. R. (2012). Settlement Obligations & the Duty of Good Faith. In *Understanding Insurance Law* (5th ed., pp. 968). New Providence, NJ: LexisNexis.

[10] Rosario, R. (2015, September). *The Status of CAMICO and the Insurance Industry*. Speech presented at Select Policyholder Luncheon, Bethesda, MD.

[11] CAMICO Insurance Co. (2007, April). Why CPAs Need Professional Liability Insurance. Retrieved January, 2016, from http://www.camico.com/blog/edit-article-why-cpas-need-professional-liability-insurance

[12] Murphy, K. M., Esq. (2016, February 5). Interview with Kevin Murphy [Telephone interview].

[13] Rosen, J., Esq., & Palmersheim, R. (2009, May 11). Using the Client Engagement Letter to Avoid CPA Malpractice Claims. Retrieved September, 2015, from http://www.cpa2biz.com/Content/media/PRODUCER_CONTENT/Newsletters/Articles_2009/CPA/May/Claims.jsp

[14] American Institute of Certified Public Accountants, Inc. (2015, October 26). AICPA Code of Professional Conduct. Retrieved December, 2015,

from http://www.aicpa.org/Research/Standards/CodeofConduct/Downloadable Documents/2014December15ContentAsof2015October26Codeof Conduct.pdf

[15] CAMICO Insurance Co. (n.d.). Frequently Asked Questions. Retrieved April, 2016, from http://www.camico.com/faq

[16] Wilck, D. S., & Shah, K. (2010, November 2). Coverage Concerns In Burning Limits Policies. Retrieved November 18, 2015, from http://www.rivkinradler.com/publications/coverage-concerns-in-burning-limits-policies/

Chapter 7 Split Limits vs. Single Limits

[1] International Risk Management Institute, Inc. (n.d.). Per Occurrence Limit. Retrieved September, 2015, from http://www.irmi.com/online/insurance-glossary/terms/p/per-occurrence-limit.aspx

[2] International Risk Management Institute, Inc. (n.d.). Aggregate Limit of Liability. Retrieved September, 2015, from http://www.irmi.com/online/insurance-glossary/terms/a/aggregate-limit-of-liability.aspx

[3] Will, D., CPA/ABV/CFF, CFE. (2015, November). *Risk Management Best Practices and Current Events*. Lecture presented at CAMICO Policyholder Luncheon, Bethesda, MD.

[4] International Risk Management Institute, Inc. (n.d.). Per Occurrence Limit. Retrieved September, 2015, from http://www.irmi.com/online/insurance-glossary/terms/p/per-occurrence-limit.aspx

[5] Affinity Insurance Services, Inc. (n.d.). Glossary. Retrieved November, 2015, from http://www.attorneys-advantage.com/sites/attorneys/service/Pages/glossary.aspx

[6] Rosario, R. (2015, September). *The Status of CAMICO and the Insurance Industry*. Speech presented at Select Policyholder Luncheon, Bethesda, MD.

[7] Rosario, R. (2015, September). *The Status of CAMICO and the Insurance Industry*. Speech presented at Select Policyholder Luncheon, Bethesda, MD.

[8] Ryles, T. (2008, October). Disclosing Policy Limits in Liability Claims: A Landmine for Bad Faith. Retrieved October, 2015, from https://www.irmi.com/articles/expert-commentary/disclosing-policy-limits-in-liability-claims-a-landmine-for-bad-faith

[9] Will, D., CPA/ABV/CFF, CFE. (2015, November). *Risk Management Best Practices and Current Events*. Lecture presented at CAMICO Policyholder Luncheon, Bethesda, MD.

[10] Cornerstone Research. (2015). Securities Class Action Settlements: 2014 Review and Analysis. Retrieved from https://www.cornerstone.com/GetAttachment/701f936e-ab1d-425b-8304-8a3e063abae8/Securities-Class-Action-Settlements-2014-Review-and-Analysis.pdf

[11] Dodsworth, J. A. (1997, September). Risk Management and High-Net-Worth Clients. *The CPA Journal*. Retrieved February, 2016, from https://www.questia.com/magazine/1P3-14022944/risk-management-and-high-net-worth-clients

[12] Rosen, J., Esq., & Palmersheim, R. (2009, May 11). Using the Client Engagement Letter to Avoid CPA Malpractice Claims. Retrieved September, 2015, from http://www.cpa2biz.com/Content/media/PRODUCER_CONTENT/Newsletters/Articles_2009/CPA/May/Claims.jsp

[13] American Institute of Certified Public Accountants, Inc. (2015, October 26). AICPA Code of Professional Conduct. Retrieved December, 2015, from

http://www.aicpa.org/Research/Standards/CodeofConduct/DownloadableDocuments/2014December15ContentAsof2015October26CodeofConduct.pdf

Chapter 8 Separate Defense Limits

[1] International Risk Management Institute, Inc. (n.d.). Defense within Limits. Retrieved September, 2015, from https://www.irmi.com/online/insurance-glossary/terms/d/defense-within-limits.aspx

[2] CAMICO. (n.d.). Separate Defense Limits vs Non-SDL Policies. Retrieved April, 2016, from https://member.camico.com/portal/LinkClick.aspx?fileticket=dUBB-aXJ8KA%3d&portalid=0

[3] Ryles, T. (2008, October). Disclosing Policy Limits in Liability Claims: A Landmine for Bad Faith. Retrieved October, 2015, from https://www.irmi.com/articles/expert-commentary/disclosing-policy-limits-in-liability-claims-a-landmine-for-bad-faith

[4] Wilck, D. S., & Shah, K. (2010, November 2). Coverage Concerns In Burning Limits Policies. Retrieved November 18, 2015, from http://www.rivkinradler.com/publications/coverage-concerns-in-burning-limits-policies/

[5] Wilck, D. S., & Shah, K. (2010, November 2). Coverage Concerns In Burning Limits Policies. Retrieved November 18, 2015, from http://www.rivkinradler.com/publications/coverage-concerns-in-burning-limits-policies/

[6] Farnham, E. (2010, May). Claims in a Recovering Economy. Retrieved February, 2016, from http://www.irmi.com/articles/expert-commentary/claims-in-a-recovering-economy

Chapter 9 Choosing a Deductible

[1] International Risk Management Institute, Inc. (n.d.). Deductible. Retrieved September, 2015, from https://www.irmi.com/online/insurance-glossary/terms/d/deductible.aspx

[2] Jerry, R. J., & Richmond, D. R. (2012). Notice of Loss Provisions. In *Understanding Insurance Law* (5th ed., pp. 577–81). New Providence, NJ: LexisNexis.

[3] Jerry, R. J., & Richmond, D. R. (2012). Notice of Loss Provisions. In *Understanding Insurance Law* (5th ed., pp. 581). New Providence, NJ: LexisNexis.

[4] Will, D., CPA/ABV/CFF, CFE. (2015, November). *Risk Management Best Practices and Current Events*. Lecture presented at CAMICO Policyholder Luncheon, Bethesda, MD.

[5] Ethridge, J. R., Marsh, T., & Revelt, B. (2007, April). Engagement Risk: Perceptions And Strategies From Audit Partners. *Journal Of Business & Economic Research*, *5*(4), 25–32.

[6] Rosario, R. (2015, September). *The Status of CAMICO and the Insurance Industry*. Speech presented at Select Policyholder Luncheon, Bethesda, MD.

[7] International Risk Management Institute, Inc. (n.d.). First Dollar Defense Coverage. Retrieved September, 2015, from http://www.irmi.com/online/insurance-glossary/terms/f/first-dollar-defense-coverage.aspx

Chapter 10 Renewing Your Professional Liability Policy

[1] International Risk Management Institute, Inc. (n.d.). Misrepresentations. Retrieved September, 2015, from https://www.irmi.com/online/insurance-glossary/terms/m/misrepresentation.aspx

[2] Company, A. M. Best (2014). Important Functions of Insurance Organizations. In *Understanding the Insurance Industry: An Overview for Those Working With and in One of the World's Most Interesting and Vital Industries* (2014 ed., pp. 7–8). AM Best Company.

[3] Fitzpatrick, Sean M., Fear is the Key: A Behavioral Guide to Underwriting Cycles. Connecticut Insurance Law Journal, Vol. 10, No. 2, pp. 255–75, 2004. Available at SSRN: http://ssrn.com/abstract=690316

[4] Jerry, R. J., & Richmond, D. R. (2012). The Insured's Duty to Pay Premiums. In *Understanding Insurance Law* (5th ed., pp. 555–69). New Providence, NJ: LexisNexis.

[5] International Risk Management Institute, Inc., *claims made and reported policy*. (n.d) retrieved April 2016, from IRMI Web Site: http://www.irmi.com/online/insurance-glossary/terms/c/claims-made-and-reported-policy.aspx

[6] Jerry, R. J., & Richmond, D. R. (2012). Notice of Loss Provisions. In *Understanding Insurance Law* (5th ed., pp. 577–81). New Providence, NJ: LexisNexis.

[7] International Risk Management Institute, Inc. (n.d.). Binder. Retrieved August, 2015, from http://www.irmi.com/online/insurance-glossary/terms/b/binder.aspx

[8] Jerry, R. J., & Richmond, D. R. (2012). The Binder. In *Understanding Insurance Law* (5th ed., pp. 199–207). New Providence, NJ: LexisNexis.

[9] Jerry, R. J., & Richmond, D. R. (2012). Delivery of the Policy. In *Understanding Insurance Law* (5th ed., pp. 208–9). New Providence, NJ: LexisNexis.

[10] International Risk Management Institute, Inc., *extended reporting period (ERP)*. (n.d) retrieved April 2016, from IRMI Web Site: https://www.irmi.com/online/insurance-glossary/terms/e/extended-reporting-period-erp.aspx

[11] Rosario, R. (2015, September). *The Status of CAMICO and the Insurance Industry*. Speech presented at Select Policyholder Luncheon, Bethesda, MD.

Chapter 11 PLI – Now What?

[1] Parker, K. M. (2008, December 1). Record Retention. *The Tax Adviser*. Retrieved January, 2016, from http://www.thetaxadviser.com/issues/2008/dec/recordretention.html

[2] Magnetic Tape to the Rescue. (2013, November 30). *The Economist*. Retrieved January, 2016, from http://www.economist.com/news/technology-quarterly/21590758-information-storage-60-year-old-technology-offers-solution-modern

[3] Transnational Auditors Committee: Forum of Firms. (2010, October). *Client Acceptance and Continuance: Good Practice Guidance* (Rep.). Retrieved February, 2016, from International Federation of Accountants website.

[4] Rosenthal, J., Esq. (2011, May 2). What's In Your Engagement Letter? Retrieved September, 2015, from http://www.cpa2biz.com/Content/media/PRODUCER_CONTENT/Newsletters/Articles_2011/CPA/may/WhatsinYourEngagementLetter.jsp

[5] Murphy, K. M., Esq. (2016, February 5). Interview with Kevin Murphy [Telephone interview].

[6] Galeck, J. J., CPA. (n.d.). Breaking Up Is Hard To Do: Disengaging Your Client. Retrieved January, 2016, from http://www.mpbf.com/news/articles/TerminatingRelationshipwithClient.pdf

[7] Platau, S., CPA, JD, & Wolfe, J. (2004, June 1). Marketing Materials and Malpractice Exposure: Advertise What Qualified to do, Not More. Retrieved February, 2016, from http://www.journalofaccountancy.com/issues/2004/jun/marketingmaterialsandmalpracticeexposure.html

[8] CAMICO Insurance Co. (n.d.). Loss Prevention Hotlines. Retrieved April, 2016, from http://www.camico.com/loss-prevention-hotlines

[9] International Risk Management Institute, Inc. (n.d.). Consent to Settlement Clause. Retrieved August, 2015, from https://www.irmi.com/online/insurance-glossary/terms/c/consent-to-settlement-clause.aspx

[10] Great American Insurance Group, Accountants Professional Liability Insurance Policy, D44100 (05/13). From http://www.landy.com/apps/Accountants/Accountants%20Policy%20Form%208-29-13%20(Specimen).pdf

[11] Marcinko, T., CPA, & Foote, B., CPA. (2010, March 1). Government Contracting. Look Before You Leap! Retrieved July, 2015, from http://www.vscpa.com/Content/58368.aspx

Chapter 12 Extended Reporting Periods/ Tail Policies (M&A)

[1] Koziel, M., CPA, CGMA. (2013, August 21). Selling Your Practice? Make Sure You Cover Your Tail. Retrieved February, 2016, from http://blog.aicpa.org/2013/08/selling-your-practice-make-sure-you-cover-your-tail.html#sthash.H22v8aaJ.dpbs

[2] International Risk Management Institute, Inc. (n.d.). Extended Reporting Period (ERP). Retrieved August, 2015, from http://www.irmi.com/online/insurance-glossary/terms/e/extended-reporting-period-erp.aspx

[3] Bregman, R. A., CPCU, RPLU, MLIS. (2002, March). Does the Discovery Provision Apply During the Extended Reporting Period? Retrieved January, 2016, from http://www.irmi.com/articles/expert-commentary/does-the-discovery-provision-apply-during-the-extended-reporting-period

[4] Rosario, R. (2015, September). *The Status of CAMICO and the Insurance Industry.* Speech presented at Select Policyholder Luncheon, Bethesda, MD

[5] Bregman, R. A., CPCU, RPLU, MLIS. (2002, March). Does the Discovery Provision Apply During the Extended Reporting Period? Retrieved January, 2016, from http://www.irmi.com/articles/expert-commentary/does-the-discovery-provision-apply-during-the-extended-reporting-period

[6] Rosario, R. (2015, September). *The Status of CAMICO and the Insurance Industry.* Speech presented at Select Policyholder Luncheon, Bethesda, MD.

[7] Pruitt, J., (Gulf Coast), & Mossman, J., (Reviewer)(Mid-Atlantic). (n.d.). *Chapter 11-Statute of Limitations* (United States, Internal Revenue Service (IRS)). Retrieved from https://www.irs.gov/pub/irs-tege/epch1102.pdf

[8] Pruitt, J., (Gulf Coast), & Mossman, J., (Reviewer)(Mid-Atlantic). (n.d.). *Chapter 11-Statute of Limitations* (United States, Internal Revenue Service (IRS)). Retrieved from https://www.irs.gov/pub/irs-tege/epch1102.pdf

[9] Pruitt, J., (Gulf Coast), & Mossman, J., (Reviewer)(Mid-Atlantic). (n.d.). *Chapter 11-Statute of Limitations* (United States, Internal Revenue Service (IRS)). Retrieved from https://www.irs.gov/pub/irs-tege/epch1102.pdf

Chapter 13 Top Five Ways to Get Sued

[1] Bryan, M., & Shapiro, R. I. (2013, October). Managing Professional Liability Litigation Against Accounting Firms (Part 1). Retrieved December, 2015, from http://www.lplegal.com/sites/default/files/CPA%20Practice%20Management%20Forum%209-13.pdf Originally Published in the CPA Practice Management Forum

[2] CAMICO Insurance Co. (July 28). 'I can't sure for fees?!' - Q&A on Lawsuits for Fees. *Impact Magazine*. Retrieved August, 2015, from http://www.camico.com/blog/impact-102-'i-can't-sue-fees'-----qa-lawsuits-fees

[3] CAMICO Insurance Co. (2009, Summer). Economy Brings Fee Issues to the Forefront. Retrieved January, 2016, from https://member.camico.com/portal/Portals/0/Reference Library/Risk Management/Fees Billing & Collections/Articles & War Stories/Economy Brings Fee Issues to the Forefront.doc

[4] CAMICO Insurance Co. (2014). Professional Liability Insurance. Retrieved March, 2016, from http://www.gbsaffinity.com/njcpa/docs/2014-CAMICO-Professional-Liabilty-Insurance-120314-GB.pdf

[5] American Institute of Certified Public Accountants, Inc. (2015, October 26). AICPA Code of Professional Conduct. Retrieved December, 2015, from http://www.aicpa.org/Research/Standards/CodeofConduct/DownloadableDocuments/2014December15ContentAsof2015October26CodeofConduct.pdf

[6] American Institute of Certified Public Accountants, Inc. (2015). AICPA Plain English guide to Independence. Retrieved from http://www.aicpa.org/interestareas/professionalethics/resources/tools/downloadabledocuments/plain_english_guide.pdf

[7] Wolfe, J., & Beckett Ference, S. (2013, October 1). Write it down: The importance of documenting oral advice. Retrieved from http://www.journalofaccountancy.com/issues/2013/oct/20138366.html

[8] Will, D. B., CPA/ABV/CFF, CFE. (2012, Fall). Professional Standards, Jury Standards, and Managing Risk. *IMPACT Magazine*, (97).

[9] Will, D. B., CPA/ABV/CFF, CFE. (2012, Fall). Professional Standards, Jury Standards, and Managing Risk. *IMPACT Magazine*, (97).

Chapter 14 Reportable Matters

[1] Jerry, R. J., & Richmond, D. R. (2012). Notice of Loss Provisions. In *Understanding Insurance Law* (5th ed., pp. 577–81). New Providence, NJ: LexisNexis.

[2] Jerry, R. J., & Richmond, D. R. (2012). Notice of Loss Provisions. In *Understanding Insurance Law* (5th ed., pp. 581). New Providence, NJ: LexisNexis.

[3] Jerry, R. J., & Richmond, D. R. (2012). Notice of Loss Provisions. In *Understanding Insurance Law* (5th ed., pp. 577–81). New Providence, NJ: LexisNexis.

[4] Jerry, R. J., & Richmond, D. R. (2012). When Notice is Due. In *Understanding Insurance Law* (5th ed., pp. 574). New Providence, NJ: LexisNexis.

[5] CAMICO Insurance Company, Accountants Professional Liability Insurance Policy, PL-1000-A (rev. 07/14). From http://www.camico.com/sites/default/files/PL-1000-A_Base%20Policy_0714%20%20%28Specimen%29.pdf

[6] Jerry, R. J., & Richmond, D. R. (2012). Notice of Loss Provisions. In *Understanding Insurance Law* (5th ed., pp. 577–81). New Providence, NJ: LexisNexis.

[7] Wells Media Group Inc. (2015, November 4). CAMICO Broadens Protection for Continuously Renewing CPA Policyholders. Retrieved November, 2015, from http://www.insurancejournal.com/news/national/2015/11/04/387414.htm

[8] Jerry, R. J., & Richmond, D. R. (2012). Notice of Loss Provisions. In *Understanding Insurance Law* (5th ed., pp. 581). New Providence, NJ: LexisNexis.

[9] HFP - Hartford Financial Products. (n.d.). Settling Without Consent - A Perilous Route. Retrieved April, 2016, from http://www.hfpinsurance.com/articles/consent.htm

[10] International Risk Management Institute, Inc. (n.d.). Consent to Settlement Clause Retrieved August, 2015, from https://www.irmi.com/online/insurance-glossary/terms/c/consent-to-settlement-clause.aspx

[11] Bernstein, W. (2005, October 3). The Ins and Outs of Claims-Made Policies. Retrieved April, 2016, from http://www.insurancejournal.com/magazines/features/2005/10/03/61167.htm

[12] Jerry, R. J., & Richmond, D. R. (2012). Notice of Loss Provisions. In *Understanding Insurance Law* (5th ed., pp. 577–81). New Providence, NJ: LexisNexis.

[13] Jerry, R. J., & Richmond, D. R. (2012). Notice of Loss Provisions. In *Understanding Insurance Law* (5th ed., pp. 577–81). New Providence, NJ: LexisNexis.

[14] Gunther, S. P., & Felsenfeld, A. D. (2014). ADR Clauses in Accounting Engagement Letters. *Dispute Resolution Journal (DRJ)*, *69*(3), 91–7. Retrieved January, 2016, from https://www.andrewskurth.com/media/article/1715_Felsenfeld_DRJ V69 _3-S Gunther _ A 2014.pdf

Chapter 15 The Fundamentals of Fraud

[1] Sheridan, T. (2015, April 21). Number of Accounting Fraud Cases Continues to Rise. Retrieved February, 2016, from http://www.accountingweb.com/aa/standards/number-of-accounting-fraud-cases-continues-to-rise

[2] Association of Certified Fraud Examiners. (2009). Occupational Fraud: A Study on the Impact of an Economic Recession. Retrieved August, 2015, from http://www.acfe.com/uploaded-Files/ACFE_Website/Content/documents/occupational-fraud.pdf

[3] Insurance Journal Broadcasting (Producer). (2009). *Failing Businesses Increase CPAs Risks* [Video file]. Retrieved January, 2016, from https://www.youtube.com/watch?v=186RBz0DVHs&feature=youtu.be

[4] Association of Certified Fraud Examiners. (2014). Report to the Nations on Occupational Fraud and Abuse: 2014 Global Fraud Study. Retrieved December, 2015, from http://www.acfe.com/rttn/docs/2014-report-to-nations.pdf

[5] CAMICO Insurance Co. (2005, February). Risk Factors and Warning Signs of Fraud. *IMPACT Magazine*. Retrieved November, 2015, from http://www.camico.com/blog/impact-103-Risk-Factors-and-Warning-Signs-of-Fraud/

[6] CAMICO Insurance Co. (2005, February). Risk Factors and Warning Signs of Fraud. *IMPACT Magazine*. Retrieved November, 2015, from http://www.camico.com/blog/impact-103-Risk-Factors-and-Warning-Signs-of-Fraud/

[7] Beckett Ference, S. (2014, February 1). Failure to detect theft and fraud: It's not just an audit issue. Retrieved March, 2015, from http://www.journalofaccountancy.com/issues/2014/feb/20139031.html

[8] Association of Certified Fraud Examiners. (2014). Report to the Nations on Occupational Fraud and Abuse: 2014 Global Fraud Study. Retrieved December, 2015, from http://www.acfe.com/rttn/docs/2014-report-to-nations.pdf

[9] Klein, R. (2015, March). How to Avoid or Minimize Fraud Exposures. *The CPA Journal*. Retrieved November, 2015, from https://www.questia.com/magazine/1P3-3663040281/how-to-avoid-or-minimize-fraud-exposures

[10] National Conference of State Legislatures. (2014, September 29). Use of Credit Information in Employment 2013 Legislation. Retrieved April, 2016, from http://www.ncsl.org/research/financial-services-and-commerce/use-of-credit-info-in-employ-2013-legis.aspx#TX

[11] OHS Health & Safety Services, Inc. (n.d.). State Drug Testing Laws. Retrieved April, 2016, from http://www.ohsinc.com/info/state-drug-testing-laws/

[12] U.S. Equal Employment Opportunity Commission. (n.d.). Background Checks: What Employers Need to Know. Retrieved March, 2016, from https://www.eeoc.gov/eeoc/publications/background_checks_employers.cfm

[13] Fraud Hotline Website. (n.d.). Retrieved April, 2016, from https://www.fraudhl.com/

This website is an example of a third party service that can be utilized by employers. Many other services exist so shop around to see what service best suits your needs.

[14] Association of Certified Fraud Examiners. (2014). Report to the Nations on Occupational Fraud and Abuse: 2014 Global Fraud Study. Retrieved December, 2015, from http://www.acfe.com/rttn/docs/2014-report-to-nations.pdf

[15] Association of Certified Fraud Examiners. (2014). Report to the Nations on Occupational Fraud and Abuse: 2014 Global Fraud Study. Retrieved December, 2015, from http://www.acfe.com/rttn/docs/2014-report-to-nations.pdf

Chapter 16 Protecting Your Firm Against Fraud Claims

[1] CAMICO Insurance Co. (n.d.). Disengagement Checklist - Recognizing Warning Signs. Retrieved February, 2016, from www.camico.com

[2] Smith, G. S., Ph.D., CPA, CMA, Hrncir, T., Ph.D., CPA, & Metts, S. (2013, January/February). Small business fraud and the trusted employee: Protecting Against Unique Vulnerabilities. Retrieved March, 2016, from http://www.acfe.com/article.aspx?id=4294976289

[3] International Risk Management Institute, Inc. (n.d.). Commercial Crime Policy. Retrieved August, 2015, from www.irmi.com/online/insurance-glossary/terms/c/commercial-crime-policy.aspx

[4] American Institute of Certified Public Accountants, Inc. (2015, June 1). Statements on Standards for Attestation Engagements. Retrieved April, 2016, from http://www.aicpa.org/Research/Standards/AuditAt-test/Pages/SSAE.aspx

[5] Public Company Accounting Board. (n.d.). Auditing Standard No. 12: Identifying and Assessing Risks of Material Misstatement. Retrieved January, 2016, from http://pcaobus.org/Standards/Auditing/Pages/Auditing_Stand-ard_12.aspx

[6] Ben Saad, E., Hoos, F., & Lesage, C. (n.d.). Why are Auditors Blamed When an Accounting Fraud is Unveiled? Experimental Evidence. Retrieved September, 2016, from http://www.nhh.no/Files/Filer/institut-ter/rrr/Seminars/2013 Ben Saad Hoos Lesage.pdf

[7] Holl, S. (2015, August). Discussing the Mitigation of Fraud Related Claims by Tailoring Engagement Letters [Telephone interview].

Executive-Team Senior Vice President of Loss Prevention Services, Holl draws on her Big Four public accounting and private industry background to provide CAMICO's policyholders with information on a wide variety of loss prevention and accounting issues. For a more in depth resource on engagement letters, consider The CPA's Guide to Effective Engagement Letters (11th Ed.)

[8] Holl, S. (2015, August). Discussing the Mitigation of Fraud Related Claims by Tailoring Engagement Letters [Telephone interview].

[9] Association of Certified Fraud Examiners. (2014). Report to the Nations on Occupational Fraud and Abuse: 2014 Global Fraud Study. Retrieved December, 2015, from http://www.acfe.com/rttn/docs/2014-report-to-nations.pdf.

Chapter 17 Loss Prevention Strategies

[1] Gunther, S. P., & Felsenfeld, A. D. (2014). ADR Clauses in Accounting Engagement Letters. *Dispute Resolution Journal (DRJ)*, *69*(3), 91–7. Retrieved January, 2016, from https://www.andrewskurth.com/media/article/1715_Felsenfeld_DRJ V69 _3-S Gunther _ A 2014.pdf

[2] American Arbitration Association. (2016, March 1). Administrative Fee Schedules (Standard and Flexible Fees). Retrieved April, 2016, from http://info.adr.org/feeschedule/

[3] Benefits of Mediation. (1998, August). Retrieved January, 2016, from http://www.mediate.com/articles/benefits.cfm

[4] Benefits of Mediation. (1998, August). Retrieved January, 2016, from http://www.mediate.com/articles/benefits.cfm

[5] Benefits of Mediation. (1998, August). Retrieved January, 2016, from http://www.mediate.com/articles/benefits.cfm

[6] Zimmerman, P. (june 1995). A practical guide to mediation for CPAs. (includes related article). *The CPA Journal.* Retrieved October, 2016, from http://archives.cpajournal.com/old/17285148.htm

[7] American Arbitration Association. (n.d.). *Non-Binding Arbitration Rules for Consumer Disputes and Business Disputes* (pp. 1–15, Rep.).

[8] The Truth Behind Mediation. (n.d.). Retrieved October, 2016, from http://www.adrr.com/adr3/other.htm

[9] Internal Revenue Service. (2006, October 30). Internal Revenue Bulletin: 2006-44, Appeals Arbitration Program. Retrieved March, 2016, from https://www.irs.gov/irb/2006-44_IRB/ar10.html

[10] American Arbitration Association. (n.d.). *Accounting and Related Services Arbitration Rules and Mediation Procedures* (pp. 1–44, Rep.).

[11] Sabater, A. (2015). Optional Appellate Arbitration Rules: Are They Good for Your Case. Retrieved December, 2015, from http://us.practical-law.com/w-000-4035

[12] American Arbitration Association. (2016, March 1). Administrative Fee Schedules (Standard and Flexible Fees). Retrieved April, 2016, from http://info.adr.org/feeschedule/

[13] American Arbitration Association. (n.d.). *Accounting and Related Services Arbitration Rules and Mediation Procedures* (pp. 1–44, Rep.).

[14] National Center for State Courts. (n.d.). Privacy/Public Access to Court Records. Retrieved April, 2016, from http://www.ncsc.org/topics/access-and-fairness/privacy-public-access-to-court-records/state-links.aspx?cat=Public Access Web Sites

[15] Smellie, R. (2013, March 12). Is Arbitration Confidential? Retrieved January, 2016, from http://www.lexology.com/library/detail.aspx?g=fe578ed6-03ca-4f77-b4f8-61094f6b901b

[16] American Arbitration Association. (n.d.). *Accounting and Related Services Arbitration Rules and Mediation Procedures* (pp. 1–44, Rep.).

[17] Sixty-Eighth Congress. (n.d.). Federal Arbitration Act. Retrieved April, 2016, from http://www.legisworks.org/congress/68/publaw-401.pdf

[18] Cornell University Law School. (n.d.). Alternative Dispute Resolution - State Laws. Retrieved March, 2016, from https://www.law.cornell.edu/wex/table_alternative_dispute_resolution

[19] Coberly, L., Johannes, T. G., Johnson, S. N., & Schaerr, G. C. (2013, March 15). United States: Supreme Court Reaffirms Congress's Strong Federal Policy Favoring Arbitration. Retrieved January, 2016, from http://www.mondaq.com/unitedstates/x/166766/Consumer Credit/Supreme Court Reaffirms Congresss Strong Federal Policy

[20] American Institute of Certified Public Accountants, Inc. (2015, October 26). AICPA Code of Professional Conduct. Retrieved December, 2015, from http://www.aicpa.org/Research/Standards/CodeofConduct/DownloadableDocuments/2014December15ContentAsof2015October26Codeof Conduct.pdf

[21] Public Company Accounting Oversight Board. (2003). ET Section 100–101. Retrieved March, 2016, from http://pcaobus.org/Standards/EI/Pages/ET101.aspx

[22] American Institute of Certified Public Accountants, Inc. (n.d.). Auditor Independence Resource Center. Retrieved February, 2016, from http://www.aicpa.org/InterestAreas/EmployeeBenefitPlanAuditQuality/Resources/AccountingandAuditingResourceCenters/AuditorIndependence/Pages/AuditorIndependenceResource Center.aspx

[23] American Institute of Certified Public Accountants, Inc. (2015, October 26). AICPA Code of Professional Conduct. Retrieved December, 2015, from http://www.aicpa.org/Research/Standards/CodeofConduct/DownloadableDocuments/2014December15ContentAsof2015October26Codeof Conduct.pdf

[24] Prendergast, K. (n.d.). Client Acceptance Procedures Best Practices Among Accounting Firms. Retrieved February, 2016, from http://www.researchassociatesinc.com/documents/BestPracticesClient.aspx

[25] CAMICO Insurance Co. (n.d.) Sample Client Screening Checklist – Corporate.

[26] Prendergast, K. (n.d.). Client Acceptance Procedures Best Practices Among Accounting Firms. Retrieved February, 2016, from http://www.researchassociatesinc.com/documents/BestPracticesClient.aspx

[27] CAMICO Insurance Co. (2004, Spring). Client Screening and Acceptance. *IMPACT Magazine*, (63).

[28] Scherzer Inrnational. (n.d.). Scherzer International Website. Retrieved February, 2016, from http://www.scherzer.com/

[29] Instant Checkmate, Inc. (n.d.). Instant Checkmate Website. Retrieved February, 2016, from https://www.instantcheckmate.com/

[30] Intelius, Inc. (n.d.). Intelius Website. Retrieved February, 2016, from http://www.intelius.com/background-check.html

[31] Weaver, P. Q., CPA, & Kulesza, M. G., CPA. (2011). Succession Planning for CPA Firm Owners: How Can CPA Societies Facilitate the Process? Retrieved January, 2016, from http://ctcpas.org/Content/Files/Pdfs/Succession Survey Report Final.pdf

[32] Wolfe, J. (2013, February 1). When parties come knocking for client records. Retrieved December, 2015, from http://www.journalofaccountancy.com/issues/2013/feb/20126773.html

[33] Cornell University Law School. (n.d.). 26 U.S. Code § 6103 - Confidentiality and disclosure of returns and return information. Retrieved March, 2016, from https://www.law.cornell.edu/uscode/text/26/6103

[34] Internal Revenue Service. (2015, December 18). Section 7216 Information Center. Retrieved January, 2016, from https://www.irs.gov/Tax-Professionals/Section-7216-Information-Center

[35] McClure, D. (2015, May 31). How to Handle the Clients From Hell. Retrieved November, 2015, from http://www.cpapracticeadvisor.com/blog/12078906/how-to-handle-the-clients-from-hell

[36] 107th Congress. (2002, July 30). PUBLIC LAW 107–204. Retrieved March, 2016, from http://www.sec.gov/about/laws/soa2002.pdf

[37] Public Company Accounting Oversight Board. (n.d.). Auditing Standard No. 3, Audit Documentation. Retrieved February, 2016, from http://pcaobus.org/Standards/Auditing/Pages/Auditing Standard 3.aspx

[38] Record Retention Guidelines. (n.d.). Retrieved March, 2016, from http://accounting-masters.com/docs/record-retention-guidelines.pdf

[39] Murphy, K. M., Esq. (2016, February 5). Interview with Kevin Murphy [Telephone interview].

[40] Ben Saad, E., Hoos, F., & Lesage, C. (n.d.). Why are Auditors Blamed When an Accounting Fraud is Unveiled? Expiremental Evidence. Retrieved September, 2016, from http://www.nhh.no/Files/Filer/institut-ter/rrr/Seminars/2013 Ben Saad Hoos Lesage.pdf

[41] For young accountants, communication is key to developing successful client relationships. (2008, September 4). Retrieved November, 2015, from http://www.accountingweb.com/practice/clients/for-young-accountants-communication-is-key-to-developing-successful-client

[42] Rosario, R. (2015). *Cpa's Guide to Effective Engagement Letters* (11th ed.). Place of publication not identified: Cch Incorporated.

Chapter 18 Employment Practices Liability Insurance Basics

[1] McMullen, D., Esq. (2010, November 1). The ABCs of Employment Practices Liability Insurance Coverage. *Risk Management Magazine*. Retrieved March, 2016, from http://www.rmmagazine.com/2010/11/01/the-abcs-of-employment-practices-liability-insurance-coverage/

[2] Richard S. Betterley, The Betterley Report, Employment Practices Liability Insurance Market Survey 2012: Rates Continue to Firm, But Not For All Carriers, December 2012 p 10.

[3] International Risk Management Institute, Inc. (n.d.). Employment Practices Liability Insurance. Retrieved September, 2015, from https://www.irmi.com/online/insurance-glossary/terms/e/employment-practices-liability-insurance-epli.aspx

[4] Mundy, J. (2011, January 5). Wrongful Termination Lawsuits on the Rise. Retrieved December, 2015, from https://www.lawyersandsettle-ments.com/articles/wrongful-termination/wrongful-termination-law-11-15747.html#.U0rd1vldWSo

[5] Hiscox Inc. (n.d.). *The 2015 Hiscox Guide to Employee Lawsuits: Employee Charge Trends Across the United States* (pp. 1–12, Rep.).

[6] Dickstein, Shapiro, Morin & Oshinsky. (2005). *A Policyholder's Primer on Insurance* (Rep.). Retrieved February, 2016, from http://www.dicksteinshapiro.com/files/upload/Insurance_Coverage_Primer_A_Policyholder's_Primer_on_Insurance.pdfhttp://www.dicksteinshapiro.com/files/upload/Insurance_Coverage_Primer_A_Policyholder's_Primer_on_Insurance.pdf

[7] Jerry, R. J., & Richmond, D. R. (2012). Particular Coverage Issues in Liability Insurance. In *Understanding Insurance Law* (5th ed., pp. 482–9). New Providence, NJ: LexisNexis.

[8] Campbell, M. (2015, June). Willful Ignorance May Not Be a Defense to Discrimination. Retrieved October, 2015, from http://www.legalsolutionsatwork.com/uncategorized/willful-ignorance-may-not-be-a-defense-to-discrimination/

[9] Leadership Conference on Civil Rights. (2001, July 1). Burden of Proof Under the Employment Non-Discrimination Act. Retrieved January, 2016, from http://www.civilrights.org/lgbt/enda/burden-of-proof.html

[10] Klenk, J. (1999). Emerging Coverage Issues in Employment Practices Liability Insurance: The Industry Perspective on Recent Developments. *Western New England Law Review, 21*(323), 323–41.

[11] Blomquist, E., Kahn, B., & Palmer, P. (2010, March 6). Employment Practices Liability Coverage: Updates and Strategies in Addressing Employment-Based Claims. Retrieved January, 2016, from http://www.mpplaw.com/files/Publication/4fa3f895-59ec-4c43-957a-f0e0c6ef3027/Presentation/PublicationAttachment/922dc81e-59f9-4c18-9213-00d2f5e07eb1/EPLI-Updates-and-Strategies.pdf

[12] Advisen Insurance Intelligence. (2014, September 18). *Complete the picture A spotlight on the United States Employment Practices Liability Insurance market* (Rep.). Retrieved November, 2015, from http://www.advisenltd.com/2014-09-18/spotlight-epli-market/

[13] Advisen Insurance Intelligence. (2014, September 18). *Complete the picture A spotlight on the United States Employment Practices Liability Insurance market* (Rep.). Retrieved November, 2015, from http://www.advisenltd.com/2014-09-18/spotlight-epli-market/

[14] Thomson Reuters. (n.d.). Trends in Employment Practice Liability. In *Employment Practice Liability: Jury Award Trends and Statistics* (2014 ed., p. 6).

[15] Thomson Reuters. (n.d.). Analysis by Defendant Type. In *Employment Practice Liability: Jury Award Trends and Statistics* (2014 ed., p. 9).

[16] Thomson Reuters. (n.d.). Analysis by Defendant Type. In *Employment Practice Liability: Jury Award Trends and Statistics* (2014 ed., p. 12).

[17] Thomson Reuters. (n.d.). A Note on Methodology. In *Employment Practice Liability: Jury Award Trends and Statistics* (2014 ed., p. 2).

[18] Seyfarth Shaw, LLP. (2015, January). 11th Annual Workplace Class Action Litigation Report. Retrieved January, 2016, from http://www.workplaceclassaction.com/files/2015/01/WCAR-Intro2.pdf

[19] Advisen Insurance Intelligence. (2014, September 18). *Complete the picture A spotlight on the United States Employment Practices Liability Insurance market* (Rep.). Retrieved November, 2015, from http://www.advisenltd.com/2014-09-18/spotlight-epli-market/

[20] Voelker, M. (2015, August 24). EPLI market update: Avoiding the sting. Retrieved October, 2015, from http://www.propertycasualty360.com/2015/08/24/epli-market-update-avoiding-the-sting?slreturn=1460413528

[21] Hiscox Inc. (n.d.). *The 2015 Hiscox Guide to Employee Lawsuits: Employee Charge Trends Across the United States* (pp. 1–12, Rep.).

[22] Blomquist, E., Kahn, B., & Palmer, P. (2010, March 6). Employment Practices Liability Coverage: Updates and Strategies in Addressing Employment-Based Claims. Retrieved January, 2016, from http://www.mpplaw.com/files/Publication/4fa3f895-59ec-4c43-957a-f0e0c6ef3027/Presentation/PublicationAttachment/922dc81e-59f9-4c18-9213-00d2f5e07eb1/EPLI-Updates-and-Strategies.pdf

[23] Ritz, P., ARM, SPHR, CRM. (2009, May 1). No surprises! High unemployment makes the case for EPLI. Retrieved September, 2015, from http://www.propertycasualty360.com/2009/05/01/no-surprises-high-unemployment-makes-the-case-for-epli

[24] U.S. Equal Employment Opportunity Commission. (n.d.). Filing a Lawsuit. Retrieved December, 2015, from https://www.eeoc.gov/employees/lawsuit.cfm

[25] Klenk, J. (1999). Emerging Coverage Issues in Employment Practices Liability Insurance: The Industry Perspective on Recent Developments. *Western New England Law Review, 21*(323), 323–41.

[26] Klenk, J. (1999). Emerging Coverage Issues in Employment Practices Liability Insurance: The Industry Perspective on Recent Developments. *Western New England Law Review, 21*(323), 323–41.

[27] Ritz, P., ARM, SPHR, CRM. (2009, May 1). No surprises! High unemployment makes the case for EPLI. Retrieved September, 2015, from http://www.propertycasualty360.com/2009/05/01/no-surprises-high-unemployment-makes-the-case-for-epli

[28] Seyfarth Shaw, LLP for the Chubb Group of Insurance Companies. (2015). Employment Practices Loss Prevention Guidelines: A Practical Guide from Chubb. Retrieved March, 2016, from http://www.chubb.com/businesses/csi/chubb2215.pdf

[29] CAMICO Insurance Co. (n.d.). CAMICO HR Support Center Website. Retrieved August, 2015, from https://camico.myhrsupportcenter.com/users/sign_in

[30] Rastagar, A. (2015, November 3). 10 Common Recruiter Questions About Background Checks. Retrieved February, 2016, from http://www.hireright.com/blog/2015/11/common-recruiter-questions-about-background-screening/

[31] Pluymert, MacDonald, Hargrove & Lee, Ltd., (2011, Aug, 29). *Why Employee Handbooks are Important.* retrieved MAR 2016, from Pluymert, MacDonald, Hargrove & Lee, LTD. Web Site: http://www.lawpmh.com/why-employee-handbooks-are-important

Chapter 19 Employment Practices Policy Specifics

[1] Thomson Reuters, (2014). *In Employment Practice Liability: Jury Award Trends and Statistics.*

[2] Seyfarth Shaw, LLP. (2015, January). 11th Annual Workplace Class Action Litigation Report. Retrieved January, 2016, from http://www.workplaceclassaction.com/files/2015/01/WCAR-Intro2.pdf

[3] Bergman, CPCU, RPLU, MLIS, Robert (2000, MAR). *Key Coverage Options under Employment Practices Liability Policies*. retrieved MAR 2016, from Internation Risk Management Institute Web Site: https://www.irmi.com/articles/expert-commentary/key-coverage-options-under-employment-practices-liability-policies

[4] Blomquist, E., Kahn, B., & Palmer, P. (2010, March 6). Employment Practices Liability Coverage: Updates and Strategies in Addressing Employment-Based Claims. Retrieved January, 2016, from http://www.mpplaw.com/files/Publication/4fa3f895-59ec-4c43-957a-f0e0c6ef3027/Presentation/PublicationAttachment/922dc81e-59f9-4c18-9213-00d2f5e07eb1/EPLI-Updates-and-Strategies.pdf

[5] Bergman, CPCU, RPLU, MLIS, Robert (2000, MAR). *Key Coverage Options under Employment Practices Liability Policies*. retrieved MAR 2016, from Internation Risk Management Institute Web Site: https://www.irmi.com/articles/expert-commentary/key-coverage-options-under-employment-practices-liability-policies

[6] Klenk, J. (1999). Emerging Coverage Issues in Employment Practices Liability Insurance: The Industry Perspective on Recent Developments. *Western New England Law Review*, *21*(323), 323–41.

[7] Seyfarth Shaw, LLP for the Chubb Group of Insurance Companies. (2015). Employment Practices Loss Prevention Guidelines: A Practical Guide from Chubb. Retrieved March, 2016, from http://www.chubb.com/businesses/csi/chubb2215.pdf

[8] Gironda, Stephanie, D. An Overview of Employment Practices Liability Insurance and Practical Considerations From a Plaintiff's Perspective. (n.d) retrieved JAN 2016, from American Bar Association Web Site: http://www.americanbar.org/content/dam/aba/events/labor_law/2013/03/employment_rightsresponsibilitiescommitteemidwinter meeting/22_gironda.authcheckdam.pdf

[9] Klenk, J. (1999). Emerging Coverage Issues in Employment Practices Liability Insurance: The Industry Perspective on Recent Developments. *Western New England Law Review*, *21*(323).

[10] Klenk, J. (1999). Emerging Coverage Issues in Employment Practices Liability Insurance: The Industry Perspective on Recent Developments. *Western New England Law Review, 21*(323), 339–41.

[11] Blomquist, E., Kahn, B., & Palmer, P. (2010, March 6). Employment Practices Liability Coverage: Updates and Strategies in Addressing Employment-Based Claims. Retrieved January, 2016, from http://www.mpplaw.com/files/Publication/4fa3f895-59ec-4c43-957a-f0e0c6ef3027/Presentation/PublicationAttachment/922dc81e-59f9-4c18-9213-00d2f5e07eb1/EPLI-Updates-and-Strategies.pdf

[12] Klenk, J. (1999). Emerging Coverage Issues in Employment Practices Liability Insurance: The Industry Perspective on Recent Developments. *Western New England Law Review, 21*(323), 330.

[13] Richard S. Betterley, The Betterley Report, Employment Practices Liability Insurance Market Survey 2012: Rates Continue to Firm, But Not For All Carriers, December 2012 pp 10.

[14] Klenk, J. (1999). Emerging Coverage Issues in Employment Practices Liability Insurance: The Industry Perspective on Recent Developments. *Western New England Law Review, 21*(323), 335.

Chapter 20 Employment Practices Policy Exclusions

[1] *Insurance Requirements & Regulations by State*. (n.d) retrieved JAN 2016, from Advanced Insurance Management, LLC Web Site: http://www.cutcomp.com/depts.htm

[2] Social Security Administration, *Benefits for People with Disabilities*. (n.d) retrieved Feb 2016, from Social Security Administration Official Website Web Site: https://www.ssa.gov/disability/

[3] United States Deparment of Labor, *Unemployment Insurance*. (n.d) retrieved MAR 2016, from United States Deparment of Labor Web Site: http://www.dol.gov/general/topic/unemployment-insurance

[4] United States Deparment of Labor, (2000, Nov, 21). *29 CFR Part 2560 Employee Retirement Income Security Act of 1974; Rules and Regulations for Administration and Enforcement; Claims Procedure; Final Rule.* retrieved DEC 2015, from United States Deparment of Labor Web Site: http://www.dol.gov/ebsa/regs/fedreg/final/2000029766.pdf

[5] *P.L. 93–406, Approved September 2, 1974 (88 Stat. 829) Employee Retirement Income Security Act of 1974.* (1974 Sep 2). retrieved Feb 2016, from Compilation of the Social Security Laws Web Site: https://www.ssa.gov/OP_Home/comp2/F093-406.html

[6] United States Congress, *National Labor Relations Act (NLRA).* (n.d) retrieved JAN 2016, from National Labor Relations Board Website Web Site: https://www.nlrb.gov/resources/national-labor-relations-act

[7] U.S. Department of Labor, *The Worker Adjustment and Retraining Notification Act: A Guide to Advance Notice of Closings and Layoffs.* (n.d) retrieved MAR 2016, from U.S. Department of Labor Employment and Training Administration: Fact Sheet Web Site: https://doleta.gov/programs/factsht/warn.htm

[8] United States Deparment of Labor, *Health Plans & Benefits: Continuation of Health Coverage - COBRA.* (n.d) retrieved Feb 2016, from United States Deparment of Labor Web Site: http://www.dol.gov/general/topic/health-plans/cobra

[9] 91st Congress, (1970, DEC, 29). *Occupational Safety and Health Act of 1970.* retrieved March 2016, from https://www.osha.gov/pls/oshaweb/owadisp.show_document?p_table=oshact&p_id=2743

[10] United States Deparment of Labor, Compliance Assistance - Wages and the Fair Labor Standards Act (FLSA). (n.d) Retrieved April 2016, from United States Deparment of Labor Web Site: http://www.dol.gov/whd/flsa/

[11] *Wage and Hour Laws by State.* (n.d) retrieved April 2016, from NOLO Web Site: http://www.nolo.com/legal-encyclopedia/wage-hour-laws-state

[12] U.S. Congress, (1963). *The Equal Pay Act of 1963.* retrieved April 2016, from U.S. Equal Employment Opportunity Commission Web Site: http://www.eeoc.gov/laws/statutes/epa.cfm

[13] United States Department of Justice: Civil Rights Division,. (n.d) retrieved April 2016, from Information and Technical Assistance on the Americans with Disabilities Act Web Site: www.ada.gov

[14] Weimer, B. D., Satre, E. D., Whitman, A. F., & Speidel, T. M. (2012). EPL Policy Coverages and Exclusion. In *Employment Practices Liability: Guide to Risk Exposures and Coverage* (p. 23). Erlanger, KY: The National Underwriter Company.

[15] Lavin H. (2010). Are Compensatory Damages Available for ADA Retaliation Claims? *employee relations law journal . 35(4)*, pp. 1–5.

[16] *Are Non-Equity Accounting Firm Partners Really Partners?* (2015, November, 16). retrieved December 2015, from CPA Practice Advisor Web Site: http://www.cpapracticeadvisor.com/news/12138876/are-non-equity-accounting-firm-partners-really-partners

Chapter 21 EPLI - Now What?

[1] Hiscox Inc. (n.d.). *The 2015 Hiscox Guide to Employee Lawsuits: Employee Charge Trends Across the United States* (pp. 1–12, Rep.).

[2] Ray, L (2013, May, 9). *How Can HR Become a Competitive Advantage for Any Organization?*. from Chron Web Site: http://smallbusiness.chron.com/can-hr-become-competitive-advantage-organization-50913.html

[3] Rastagar, A. (2015, November 3). 10 Common Recruiter Questions About Background Checks. Retrieved February, 2016, from http://www.hireright.com/blog/2015/11/common-recruiter-questions-about-background-screening/

[4] U.S. Equal Employment Opportunity Commission, *Pre-Employment Inquiries and Arrest & Conviction*. (n.d) retrieved December 2015, from Employment Opportunity Commission Web Site: http://www.eeoc.gov/laws/practices/inquiries_arrest_conviction.cfm

[5] Federal Trade Commission, *Using Consumer Reports: What Employers Need to Know*. (n.d) retrieved April 2016, from Federal Trade Commission Web Site: https://www.ftc.gov/tips-advice/business-center/guidance/using-consumer-reports-what-employers-need-know

[6] *Drug Testing Laws by State.* (2004, April). from TestCountry.com Web Site: http://www.testcountry.com/StateLaws/

[7] iCIMS, *Onboarding Automating the Onboarding Process to Realize Significant Return on Investment.* (n.d) retrieved April 2016, from https://www.icims.com/sites/www.icims.com/files/public/Onboarding%20ROI%20White%20Paper_9_2014.pdf

[8] CAMICO Insurance Co. (n.d) retrieved April 2016, from CAMICO HR Support Web Site: https://camico.myhrsupportcenter.com/app/button/3

[9] *Employee Handbooks.* (n.d) retrieved March 2016, from U.S. Small Business Administration Web Site: https://www.sba.gov/starting-business/hire-retain-employees/employee-handbooks

[10] Pluymert, MacDonald, Hargrove & Lee, Ltd., (2011, Aug, 29). *Why Employee Handbooks are Important.* retrieved MAR 2016, from Pluymert, MacDonald, Hargrove & Lee, LTD. Web Site: http://www.lawpmh.com/why-employee-handbooks-are-important

[11] CAMICO Insurance Co., *Employee Handbook Wizard.* (n.d) retrieved April 2016, from CAMICO HR Support Web Site: https://camico.myhrsupportcenter.com/app/handbooks/new

[12] Meyer, E. B. (2014, May, 15). *PA Superior Court closes non-competition-agreement loophole.* retrieved March 2016, from The Employer Handbook Web Site: http://www.theemployerhandbook.com/2014/05/pa-superior-court-closes-non-c.html

[13] *Employers Beware: Your Employee Handbook's Arbitration Clause May Not be Enforceable.* (n.d) retrieved March 2016, from Michel & Associates, P.C. Attorneys at Law Web Site: http://michellawyers.com/employers-beware-your-employee-handbooks-arbitration-clause-may-not-be-enforceable/

[14] *5 Goals of Employee Performance Evaluation: Why Organizations Do Employee Performance Evaluation.* (n.d) retrieved March 2016, from AboutMoney Web Site: http://humanresources.about.com/od/performancemanagement/qt/employee_evaluation.htm

[15] *Use Disciplinary Actions Effectively and Legally: How to Take Effective, Legal Disciplinary Actions With Employees.* (n.d) retrieved March 2016, from AboutMoney Web Site: http://humanresources.about.com/od/discipline/qt/disciplinary-actions.htm

[16] CAMICO Insurance Co. (n.d) retrieved April 2016, from Termination Checklist Web Site: https://camico.myhrsupportcenter.com/app/landing/26/content/1123

[17] Seyfarth Shaw, LLP for the Chubb Group of Insurance Companies. (2015). Employment Practices Loss Prevention Guidelines: A Practical Guide from Chubb. Retrieved March, 2016, from http://www.chubb.com/businesses/csi/chubb2215.pdf

[18] CAMICO Insurance Co., (n.d) retrieved April 2016, from Employment Practices Liability Insurance Brochure Web Site: http://www.camico.com/sites/default/files/2015-Employment%20Practices%20Liability-042815.pdf

Chapter 22 Employment Practices Risk Reduction Measures

[1] National Conference of State Legislatures, *Employment At-Will Exceptions by State.* (n.d) retrieved March 2016, from National Conference of State Legislatures Web Site: http://www.ncsl.org/research/labor-and-employment/at-will-employment-exceptions-by-state.aspx

[2] Vu, N. (2015, August 6). Questions Concerning EPLI Insurance Policies and Generally Recommended HR Practices. [Telephone interview].

Natalie Vu is a Professional Liability Claims Specialist at CAMICO Mutual Insurance Company, as well as a lawyer registered with the State Bar of California

[3] Enos, R. (2011, May, 11). *Are Employee Handbooks Enforceable Contracts?.* retrieved JAN 2016, from FindLaw Web Site: http://blogs.findlaw.com/free_enterprise/2011/05/are-employee-handbooks-enfrceable-contracts.html

[4] Vu, N. (2015, August 6). Questions Concerning EPLI Insurance Policies and Generally Recommended HR Practices. [Telephone interview].

5 Corrigan W.M. (2006). Non-Compete Agreements and Unfair Competition – An Updated Overview. *Journal of The Missouri Bar.*, 81–90.

6 Bussing, H. (2011, June, 1). *Is Your Non-compete Agreement Enforceable.* retrieved JAN 2016, from HRExaminer Web Site: http://www.hrexaminer.com/is-your-non-compete-agreement-enforceable/

7 Seyfarth Shaw, LLP for the Chubb Group of Insurance Companies. (2015). Employment Practices Loss Prevention Guidelines: A Practical Guide from Chubb. Retrieved March, 2016, from http://www.chubb.com/businesses/csi/chubb2215.pdf

8 Vu, N. (2015, August 6). Questions Concerning EPLI Insurance Policies and Generally Recommended HR Practices. [Telephone interview].

9 Thomas, J.D., R. (2009, November, 9). *Definitions of Employee Classifications.* retrieved January 2016, from PayScale: Human Capital Web Site: http://www.payscale.com/compensation-today/2009/11/definitions-of-employee-classifications

10 United States Deparment of Labor, *Wages.* (n.d) retrieved February 2016, from United States Deparment of Labor Web Site: http://www.dol.gov/dol/topic/wages/index.htm

Chapter 23 Four Myths of Cyber Insurance

1 *Cybercrime - No One Is Immune.* (2011, December, 7). retrieved January 2016, from AccountingWeb Web Site: http://www.accountingweb.com/aa/law-and-enforcement/cybercrime-no-one-is-immune

2 Harman, P.L. (2015, October, 7). *50% of small businesses have been the target of a cyber attack.* retrieved October 07 2015, from PropertyCasualty360 Web Site: http://www.propertycasualty360.com/2015/10/07/50-of-small-businesses-have-been-the-target-of-a-c?slreturn=1460472649

3 Kaspersky, E. (2011, October, 2011). *Number of the Month: 70K per Day..* retrieved January 2016, from Nota Bene: Notes Comment and Buzz from Eugene Kaspersky - Official Blog Web Site: https://eugene.kaspersky.com/2011/10/28/number-of-the-month-70k-per-day/

[4] Waldron, A. & Halstrom, D. (2013, August, 01). *A breach of client data: Risks to CPA firms*. retrieved March 2016, from Journal of Accountancy Web Site: http://www.journalofaccountancy.com/issues/2013/aug/20138003.html

[5] Association of Chartered Certified Accountants, (2016, Feb). *Cybersecurity – Fighting Crime's Enfant Terrible*. retrieved March 2016, from Future Today Web Site: http://www.futuretoday.com/content/dam/IMA/pdf/Technology/Digital/ACCA-IMA-Cybersecurity%20Report%20v8.pdf

[6] Boyd, A. (2015, June, 25). Contractor breach gave hackers keys to OPM data. retrieved January 2016, from Federal Times Web Site: http://www.federaltimes.com/story/government/omr/opm-cyber-report/2015/06/23/keypoint-usis-opm-breach/28977277/

[7] Schwartz, M. J. (2011, May, 30). *Lockheed Martin Suffers Massive Cyberattack*. retrieved December 2015, from InformationWeek: DarkReading Web Site: http://www.darkreading.com/risk-management/lockheed-martin-suffers-massive-cyberattack/d/d-id/1098013

[8] Samson, T. (2012, August, 08). *Malware infects 30 percent of computers in U.S: Report shows U.S. has eighth-highest PC malware rate among developed countries, examines new 'ransomware' that hijacks Web cams.*. retrieved January 2016, from InfoWorld Web Site: http://www.infoworld.com/article/2618043/cybercrime/malware-infects-30-percent-of-computers-in-u-s-.html

[9] Ponemon Institute & IBM, (2016). *Data Breach Risk Calculator*. retrieved April 2016, from IBM Data Breach Risk Calculator Web Site: http://ibmcostofdatabreach.com/

[10] Weissman, C.G. (2015, July, 14). *Some hackers make more than $80,000 a month – here's how*. retrieved December 2015, from Business Insider Web Site: http://www.businessinsider.com/we-found-out-how-much-money-hackers-actually-make-2015-7

[11] Weissman, C.G. (2015, July, 14). *Some hackers make more than $80,000 a month – here's how*. retrieved December 2015, from Business Insider Web Site: http://www.businessinsider.com/we-found-out-how-much-money-hackers-actually-make-2015-7

[12] Weissman, C.G. (2015, July, 14). *Some hackers make more than $80,000 a month – here's how.* retrieved December 2015, from Business Insider Web Site: http://www.businessinsider.com/we-found-out-how-much-money-hackers-actually-make-2015-7

[13] *Statement Before the Senate Judiciary Committee, Subcommittee on Crime and Terrorism* (2011) (testimony of Gordon M. Snow Assistant Director, Cyber Division Federal Bureau of Investigation).

retrieved from: https://www.fbi.gov/news/testimony/cybersecurity-responding-to-the-threat-of-cyber-crime-and-terrorism

[14] Gordon, L.A. & Loeb, M.P. (2002, November). The Economics of Information Security Investment. *ACM Transactions on Information and System Security, 5(4)*, 438–57.

[15] National Cyber Security Alliance, *Small Business Online Security Infographic.* (n.d) retrieved January 2016, from StaySafeOnline.Org Web Site: https://staysafeonline.org/business-safe-online/resources/small-business-online-security-infographic

[16] *Statement before the House Financial Services Committee, Subcommittee on Financial Institutions and Consumer Credit* (2011) (testimony of Gordon M. Snow Assistant Director, Cyber Division Federal Bureau of Investigation). retrieved from: https://www.fbi.gov/news/testimony/cyber-security-threats-to-the-financial-sector

[17] Hadnagy, C. (2011). *Social Engineering: The Art of Human Hacking.* Indianapolis, IN: Wiley Publishing Inc.

[18] *Before the United States House of Representatives Subcommittee on Financial Institutions and Consumer Credit "Fighting Identity Theft – The Role of FCRA"* (2003) (testimony of Joseph Ansanelli Chairman and CEO of Vontu, Inc.). retrieved from: http://financialservices.house.gov/media/pdf/062403ja.pdf

[19] Rosen, M. (2009, March, 5). *Report: Employee Theft of Information is Pervasive.* retrieved March 2016, from Massachusetts Noncompete Law Web Site: http://www.massachusettsnoncompetelaw.com/2009/03/report-employee-theft-of-information-is-pervasive/

[20] Rosen, M. (2009, March, 5). *Report: Employee Theft of Information is Pervasive.* retrieved March 2016, from Massachusetts Noncompete Law Web Site: http://www.massachusettsnoncompetelaw.com/2009/03/report-employee-theft-of-information-is-pervasive/

[21] Kelly, E. (2014, October, 20). *Officials warn 500 million financial records hacked.* retrieved December 2015, from USA Today Web Site: http://www.usatoday.com/story/news/politics/2014/10/20/secret-service-fbi-hack-cybersecuurity/17615029/

Chapter 24 Cyber Insurance Policy Specifics

[1] Hiscox Inc. (2014). *Hiscox Technology, Privacy and Cyber Protection Portfolio* (pp. 1–4, Rep.). Hiscox. Retrieved from: http://www.hiscox-broker.com/shared-documents/9894_us_tech_privacy_cyber_protection_portfolio_factsheet.pdf

[2] International Risk Management Institute, Inc. (n.d.). Self-Insured Retention (SIR). Retrieved September, 2015, from http://www.irmi.com/online/insurance-glossary/terms/s/self-insured-retention-sir.aspx

[3] National Conference of State Legislatures. (2016, April 1). Security Breach Notification Laws. Retrieved April, 2016, from http://www.ncsl.org/research/telecommunications-and-information-technology/security-breach-notification-laws.aspx

[4] Ponemon Institute LLC. (2014, September). *Is Your Company Ready for a Big Data Breach? The Second Annual Study on Data Breach Preparedness* (Rep.). Retrieved January, 2016, from Experian® Data Breach Resolution website: http://www.experian.com/assets/data-breach/brochures/2014-ponemon-2nd-annual-preparedness.pdf

[5] Zurich American Insurance Corp. (2011, September). *Data Breach Cost; Part one: Risks, costs and mitigation strategies for data breaches* (Rep.). Retrieved January, 2016, from Zurich American Insurance Corporation website: http://www.experian.com/assets/data-breach/brochures/2014-ponemon-2nd-annual-preparedness.pdf

[6] Zurich American Insurance Corp. (2011, September). *Data Breach Cost; Part one: Risks, costs and mitigation strategies for data breaches* (Rep.). Retrieved January, 2016, from Zurich American Insurance Corporation website: http://www.experian.com/assets/data-breach/brochures/2014-ponemon-2nd-annual-preparedness.pdf

[7] Zurich American Insurance Corp. (2011, September). *Data Breach Cost; Part one: Risks, costs and mitigation strategies for data breaches* (Rep.). Retrieved January, 2016, from Zurich American Insurance Corporation website: http://www.experian.com/assets/data-breach/brochures/2014-ponemon-2nd-annual-preparedness.pdf

[8] Vormetric Data Security. (2015). *2015 Insider Threat Report* (Rep.). Retrieved March, 2016, from Vormetric Data Security website: http://www.vormetric.com/campaigns/insiderthreat/2015/

[9] Halsey, R. (2009, April, 16). *The Real Cost of Data Breach.* retrieved January 2016, from ComplianceGuide.org Web Site: https://www.pcicomplianceguide.org/the-real-cost-of-data-breach/

[10] Philadelphia Indemnity Insurance Company, Cyber Security Liability Coverage Form, PI-CYB-001 (08/12). From https://www.phly.com/Files/PI-CYB-001%20(08-12)%20Cyber%20Security%20Liability%20Coverage%20Form31-932.pdf

[11] Hern, A. (2014, June, 3). Cryptolocker: what you need to know. retrieved April 2016, from The Guardian Web Site: https://www.theguardian.com/technology/2014/jun/03/cryptolocker-what-you-need-to-know

[12] Unk., Paul (2015, October, 22). *FBI's Advice on Ransomware? Just Pay The Ransom..* retrieved December 2015, from The Security Ledger Web Site: https://securityledger.com/2015/10/fbis-advice-on-cryptolocker-just-pay-the-ransom/

Chapter 25 Cyber Insurance Exclusions

[1] Brickey, J. (2012, August, 23). *Defining Cyberterrorism: Capturing a Broad Range of Activities in Cyberspace.* retrieved December 2015, from Combating Terrorism Center Web Site: https://www.ctc.usma.edu/posts/defining-cyberterrorism-capturing-a-broad-range-of-activities-in-cyberspace

[2] An Act, To Extend The Terrorism Insurance Program of The Department of The Treasury, and for Other Purposes, December 26, 2007, Public Law 110-160, U.S. Government Printing Office – 2008. From: https://www.gpo.gov/fdsys/pkg/PLAW-110publ160/html/PLAW-110publ160.htm

[3] LaCroix, K. (2015, July, 15). *Guest Post: Cyber & Privacy Policy Exclusions: Analyzing Differences, Negotiating Modifications.* retrieved April 2016, from The D&O Diary: A Periodic Journal Containing Items of Interest From the World of Directors & Officers Liability, With Occasional Commentary Web Site: http://www.dandodiary.com/2015/07/articles/cyber-liability/guest-post-cyber-privacy-policy-exclusions-analyzing-differences-negotiating-modifications/

[4] Minor, J. (2015, June, 24). *Ransomware on the Rise.* retrieved January 2016, from PCMag Web Site: http://www.pcmag.com/article2/0,2817,2486586,00.asp

Chapter 26 Cyber Incident Roadmap

[1] Business Insurance, (2014, October, 1). *Business insurance.* retrieved December 2015, from Cyber breaches inevitable; business leaders advised to be prepared Web Site: http://www.businessinsurance.com/article/20141001/NEWS08/141009987

[2] Meola, A. (2016, March, 03). *A major red flag about security could threaten the entire IoT.* retrieved April 2016, from Business Insider: Business Intelligence Web Site: http://www.businessinsider.com/iot-cyber-security-hacking-problems-internet-of-things-2016-3

[3] Heyman, A. (2014, January, 20). *Does Your Firm Have a Data Breach Response Plan?* retrieved January 2016, from CPA Practice Advisor Web Site: http://www.cpapracticeadvisor.com/news/11297155/does-your-firm-have-a-data-breach-response-plan

[4] Ponemon Institute. (2013, February). *The Post Breach Boom* (Rep.). Retrieved December, 2015, from Solera Networks website: http://www.ponemon.org/local/upload/file/Post Breach Boom V7.pdf

[5] Smith, G. (2014, October, 23). *Hackers Ran Loose Inside JPMorgan For 2 Months Before Getting Caught*. retrieved November 2015, from HuffPost Business Web Site: http://www.huffingtonpost.com/2014/10/23/jpmorgan-hackers_n_6029266.html

[6] Farhat, V. McCarthy, B., & Raysman, R. (2011). *Cyber Attacks: Prevention and Proactive Responses*. retrieved February 2016, from HKLaw Web Site: https://www.hklaw.com/files/Publication/bd9553c5-284f-4175-87d2-849aa07920d3/Presentation/PublicationAttachment/1880b6d6-eae2-4b57-8a97-9f4fb1f58b36/CyberAttacksPreventionandProactiveResponses.pdf

[7] Federal Bureau of Investigation. (n.d) retrieved April 2016, from Cyber Crime Investigation Website Web Site: https://www.fbi.gov/about-us/investigate/cyber/cyber

[8] Department of Homeland Security, *United States Secret Service Electronic Crimes Task Forces*. (n.d) retrieved April 2016, from Department of Homeland Security Web Site: https://www.dhs.gov/sites/default/files/publications/USSS%20Electronic%20Crimes%20Task%20Force.pdf

[9] Department of Homeland Security, (2016, January, 8). *Combating Cyber Crime*. retrieved January 2016, from Homeland Security Web Site: https://www.dhs.gov/topic/combating-cyber-crime

[10] StorageCraft Technology Corporation, (2011). *Building Your Backup and Disaster Recovery Plan 101*. retrieved October 2015, from StorageCraft Web Site: https://www.storagecraft.com/documents/Building-a-BDR-Plan-101-final.pdf

[11] National Conference of State Legislatures. (2016, April 1). Security Breach Notification Laws. Retrieved April, 2016, from http://www.ncsl.org/research/telecommunications-and-information-technology/security-breach-notification-laws.aspx

[12] *What is a Penetration Test and Why Would I Need One for My Company*. (2013, October, 13). retrieved July 2015, from Forbes Web Site: http://www.forbes.com/sites/ericbasu/2013/10/13/what-is-a-penetration-test-and-why-would-i-need-one-for-my-company/#5358014e42da

[13] Reynolds, S. E. (2015, August, 28). *Evaluating the Severity of a Data Breach.* retrieved December 2015, from IceMiller Web Site: http://www.icemiller.com/blogs/ice-miller-blog/april-2015/evaluating-the-severity-of-a-data-breach/

[14] Zetter, K. (2015, September, 17). *Hacker Lexicon: A Guide to Ransomware, the Scary Hack That's on the Rise.* retrieved November 2015, from Wired Web Site: http://www.wired.com/2015/09/hacker-lexicon-guide-ransomware-scary-hack-thats-rise/

[15] National Conference of State Legislatures. (2016, April 1). Security Breach Notification Laws. Retrieved April, 2016, from http://www.ncsl.org/research/telecommunications-and-information-technology/security-breach-notification-laws.aspx

[16] US-CERT: United States Computer Emergency Readiness Team, (2009, November, 04). *Security Tip (ST04-015) Understanding Denial-of-Service Attacks.* retrieved March 2016, from Department of Homeland Security Web Site: https://www.us-cert.gov/ncas/tips/ST04-015

[17] DOJ Cybersecurity Unit, (2015, April). *Best Practices for Victim Response and Reporting of Cyber Incidents.* retrieved December 2015, from Department of Justice Web Site: ttps://www.justice.gov/sites/default/files/opa/speeches/attachments/2015/04/29/criminal_division_guidance_on_best_practices_for_victim_response_and_reporting_cyber_incidents2.pdf

[18] DOJ Cybersecurity Unit, (2015, April). *Best Practices for Victim Response and Reporting of Cyber Incidents.* retrieved December 2015, from Department of Justice Web Site: ttps://www.justice.gov/sites/default/files/opa/speeches/attachments/2015/04/29/criminal_division_guidance_on_best_practices_for_victim_response_and_reporting_cyber_incidents2.pdf

[19] Thompson, C. (2016, February, 21). *Why you should never pay hackers if they take over your computer.* retrieved February 2016, from Business insider: Tech Insider Web Site: http://www.businessinsider.com/why-you-shouldnt-pay-ransomware-hackers-2016-2

20 Balestrat, M. (2015, September, 14). *What's A Zero Day? (And Why Should You Care?)*. retrieved December 2015, from BreachAlarm Web Site: https://blog.breachalarm.com/what-is-a-zero-day-and-why-should-i-care

Chapter 27 Cyber Risk Reduction Measures

1 CBR Staff Writer, (2015, September, 02). *Data breaches - hackers have nothing on your own employees*. retrieved December 2015, from Computer Business Review Web Site: http://www.cbronline.com/news/cybersecurity/business/data-breaches---hackers-have-nothing-on-your-own-employees-4660652

2 ISACA, (2010). *Audit/Assurance Program: Mobile Computing Security*. retrieved January 2016, from Information Systems Audit and Control Association, Inc. Web Site: https://www.isaca.org/bookstore/Pages/Product-Detail.aspx?Product_code=WAPMCS

3 Globalsign. (n.d.). *S/MIME Certificates: The benefits and best practices of secure email signature and encryption* (Rep.). Retrieved December, 2015, from Globalsign website: https://www.globalsign.com/files/7814/3591/1111/whitepaper-smime-benefits-and-best-practices.pdf

4 SANS institute. (2001). *System Administrator - Security Best Practices* (Rep.). Retrieved December, 2015, from SANS Institute InfoSec Reading Room website: https://www.sans.org/reading-room/whitepapers/bestprac/system-administrator-security-practices-657

5 Shinder, D. (2007, July, 16). *10 physical security measures every organization should take*. retrieved November 2015, from TechRepublic Web Site: http://www.techrepublic.com/blog/10-things/10-physical-security-measures-every-organization-should-take/

6 Mah, P. (2013, October, 1). *4 ways to disaster-proof your data backups*. retrieved January 2016, from PCWorld Web Site: http://www.pcworld.com/article/2050337/5-ways-to-disaster-proof-your-data-backups.html

Chapter 28 RIA Insurance Basics

[1] American Institute of Certified Public Accountants, Inc. (2015). *The CPA's Guide to Investment Advisory Business: Models have you crossed the Line When providing Investment Advice?* (Rep.). Retrieved February, 2016, from American Institute of Certified Public Accountants website: http://www.aicpa.org/InterestAreas/PersonalFinancialPlanning/Resources/PFPPracticeManagement/PFPPracticeGuides/DownloadableDocuments/CPA-guide-investment.pdf

[2] Investopedia, *Viatical Settlement.* (n.d) retrieved March 2016, from Investopedia Web Site: http://www.investopedia.com/terms/v/viaticalsettlement.asp

[3] CAMICO Insurance Co., Financial Services Endorsement, PL-1042-A (04/09).

[4] Multpl.com. (2016, April 29). S&P 500 Historical Prices by Year. Retrieved April, 2016, from http://www.multpl.com/s-p-500-historical-prices/table/by-year

[5] Financial Industry Regulation Authority. (2016, March). Dispute Resolution Statistics. Retrieved April 30, 2016, from http://www.finra.org/arbitration-and-mediation/dispute-resolution-statistics

[6] CAMICO Insurance Co., Financial Services Endorsement, PL-1042-A (04/09).

[7] Florian, G. M. (2016, February 14). State of Accountants' Professional Liability Industry [Telephone interview].

[8] Bigelow, III, B (2006). *What E&O Limit Should You Purchase?* retrieved August, 2015, from Markel Insurance Web Site: http://www.markelinsurance.com/~/media/specialty/investment-advisors/risk-manangement-pdf-articles/what-eo-limit-should-you-purchase.pdf?la=en

[9] Markel Investment Advisors, *About Us.* (n.d) retrieved February 2016, from Markel Insurance Co. Web Site: http://www.markelinvestmentadvisors.com/about-us

10 Company, A. M. (2014). Important Functions of Insurance Organizations. In *Understanding the Insurance Industry: An Overview for Those Working With and in One of the World's Most Interesting and Vital Industries* (2014 ed., pp. 7–9). AM Best Company.

11 RIA in a Box, (2014, May, 04). *Registered Investment Adviser (RIA) Errors and Omissions Insurance.* retrieved December 2015, from RIA in a Box Web Site: http://www.riainabox.com/blog/registered-investment-adviser-ria-errors-and-omissions-insurance

Chapter 29 Narrowing Down RIA Insurers

1 Markel Insurance Company, *Important Questions to Ask.* (n.d) retrieved April 2016, from Markel Investment Advisors Web Site: http://www.markelinvestmentadvisors.com/faq

2 Severinghaus, G. (2016, January). Status of Markel RIA Insurance & The Industry as a Whole [Telephone interview].

Greg serves as Marketing Manager and Underwriter for Markel Cambridge Alliance and has been with Markel since February 2011. Prior to Markel, Greg has over 10 years of Financial Services experience, an undergraduate degree in economics from the University of Puget Sound and an MBA from William & Mary. Greg has significant business experience with American Funds, Paychex, MassMutual, and a third party 401k administrator

Chapter 30 RIA Policy Specifics & Exclusions

1 Bigelow, III, B (2006). *What E&O Limit Should You Purchase?* retrieved August, 2015, from Markel Insurance Web Site: http://www.markelinsurance.com/~/media/specialty/investment-advisors/risk-manangement-pdf-articles/what-eo-limit-should-you-purchase.pdf?la=en

2 McCullough, Campbell & Lane, LLC. (n.d.). Jurisdictional Analysis (of punitive damages by state). Retrieved February, 2016, from http://www.mcandl.com/puni_states.html

[3] American Arbitration Association, (2016, March, 1). *Administrative Fee Schedules (Standard and Flexible Fees)*. retrieved March 2016, from American Bar Association Web Site: http://info.adr.org/feeschedule/

[4] Financial Industry Regulatory Authority, (2016). Dispute Resolution Statistics. retrieved March 2016, from FINRA Web Site: http://www.finra.org/arbitration-and-mediation/dispute-resolution-statistics

Chapter 31 What Minimum Limits Should I Carry?

[1] Financial Industry Regulatory Authority. (2016). Statistics. Retrieved April 23, 2016, from http://www.finra.org/newsroom/statistics

[2] Securities Arbitration Commentator. (2007, August). 2006 Annual Award Survey: A SAC Award Survey Comparing Results in 2006 to 2000–2005. *Securities Arbitration Commentator*. Retrieved March, 2016, from http://www.sacarbitration.com/pdf/2006 Annual Award Survey.pdf

[3] Securities Arbitration Commentator. (2007, August). 2006 Annual Award Survey: A SAC Award Survey Comparing Results in 2006 to 2000–2005. *Securities Arbitration Commentator*. Retrieved March, 2016, from http://www.sacarbitration.com/pdf/2006 Annual Award Survey.pdf

[4] Will, D., CPA/ABV/CFF, CFE. (2015, November). *Risk Management Best Practices and Current Events*. Lecture presented at CAMICO Policyholder Luncheon, Bethesda, MD.

[5] Bigelow, III, B (2006). *What E&O Limit Should You Purchase?* retrieved August, 2015, from Markel Insurance Web Site: http://www.markelinsurance.com/~/media/specialty/investment-advisors/risk-manangement-pdf-articles/what-eo-limit-should-you-purchase.pdf?la=en

[6] Bigelow, III, B (2006). *What E&O Limit Should You Purchase?* retrieved August, 2015, from Markel Insurance Web Site: http://www.markelinsurance.com/~/media/specialty/investment-advisors/risk-manangement-pdf-articles/what-eo-limit-should-you-purchase.pdf?la=en

[7] Investopedia Staff, *Determining Risk And The Risk Pyramid*. (n.d) retrieved March 2016, from Investopedia Web Site: investopedia.com/articles/basics/03/050203.asp

[8] Severinghaus, G. (2016, January). Status of Markel RIA Insurance & The Industry as a Whole [Telephone interview].

[9] Bigelow, III, B (2006). *What E&O Limit Should You Purchase?*. retrieved August, 2015, from Markel Insurance Web Site: http://www.markelinsurance.com/~/media/specialty/investment-advisors/risk-manangement-pdf-articles/what-eo-limit-should-you-purchase.pdf?la=en

[10] Bigelow, III, B (2006). *What E&O Limit Should You Purchase?*. retrieved August, 2015, from Markel Insurance Web Site: http://www.markelinsurance.com/~/media/specialty/investment-advisors/risk-manangement-pdf-articles/what-eo-limit-should-you-purchase.pdf?la=en

[11] Severinghaus, G. (2016, January). Status of Markel RIA Insurance & The Industry as a Whole [Telephone interview].

[12] RIA in a Box, (2014, May, 04). *Registered Investment Adviser (RIA) Errors and Omissions Insurance*. retrieved January 2016, from RIA Compliance and Practice Management Blog Web Site: http://www.riainabox.com/blog/registered-investment-adviser-ria-errors-and-omissions-insurance

Chapter 32 RIA Risk Reduction Measures

[1] RIA in a Box, (2014, April, 12). *How to choose an RIA Compliance Consultant*. retrieved January 2016, from RIA Compliance and Practice Management Blog Web Site: http://www.riainabox.com/blog/how-to-choose-an-ria-compliance-consultant

[2] Baird's Advisory Services Research, (2012). *The Hidden Cost of Holding a Concentrated Position: Why diversification can help to protect wealth*. retrieved January 2016, from RWBaird Web Site: http://www.rwbaird.com/bolimages/Media/PDF/Whitepapers/Hidden-Cost-Holding-Concentrated-Position.pdf

[3] Markel Insurance Co. (2011, Spring). Risk Management News: For Investment Advisors. Retrieved August, 2015, from
http://www.markelinsurance.com/~/media/specialty/investment-advisors/risk-manangement-pdf-articles/cambridgermn_spring2011.pdf?la=en

[4] Financial West Group, (2016, March, 18). *Financial West Group: RIA Adviser Managed Accounts Program (AMAP) Internal Policy and Procedures.* retrieved April 2016, from Financial West Group Web Site:
https://www.fwg.com/wp-content/uploads/2014/11/RIA-Internal-Policy-and-Procedures-Quick-Reference-Matrix.pdf

[5] NASAA, (2011, September, 11). *NASAA Recordkeeping Requirements For Investment Advisers Model Rule 203(a)-2.* retrieved February 2016, from North American Securities Administrators Association Web Site:
http://www.nasaa.org/wp-content/uploads/2011/07/IA-Model-Rule-Recordkeeping.pdf

[6] Hill, B. (2013, February, 12). *Qualifications of a Chief Compliance Officer.* retrieved January 2016, from RIA Compliance Consultants Web Site:
http://www.ria-compliance-consultants.com/the_regulatory_maze/2013/02/qualifications-of-a-chief-compliance-officer/

[7] Securities and Exchange Commission, (2011, August, 12). *Implementation of the Whistleblower Provisions of Section 21F of the Securities Exchange Act of 1934, 17 CFR Parts 240 and 249 [Release No. 34-64545; File No. S7-33-10] RIN 3235-AK78.* retrieved January 2016, from SEC Web Site:
https://www.sec.gov/rules/final/2011/34-64545.pdf

[8] Giachetti, T. D. (2012, March, 01). *Are You Fulfilling Your 'Mandatory' Training Requirement? While firms aren't explicitly required to provide employee training, the SEC is looking for a culture of compliance.* retrieved November 2015, from Think Advisor Web Site: http://www.thinkadvisor.com/2012/03/01/are-you-fulfilling-your-mandatory-training-require?slreturn=1460598322

[9] Financial Industry Regulatory Authority, (2012). *What to Expect: FINRA's Dispute Resolution Process.* retrieved January 2016, from FINRA Web Site:
http://www.finra.org/sites/default/files/Education/p117487_0_0.pdf

[10] Financial Industry Regulatory Authority, (2016). *Arbitration Overview*. retrieved March 2016, from FINRA Web Site: https://www.finra.org/arbitration-and-mediation/arbitration-overview

[11] Markel Cambridge Alliance, (2014). *Investment Advisors: Risk Management Tips*. retrieved January 2016, from Markel Cambridge Alliance Web Site: http://www.markelinsurance.com/~/media/specialty/investment-advisors/risk-manangement-pdf-articles/alternative-dispute-resolution.pdf?la=en

Chapter 33 Tips on Minimizing Wire Fraud

[1] FA Staff, (2013, October, 28). RIA Fined By SEC After Hacker Uses E-Mails To Steal Client Funds. retrieved January 2016, from Financial Advisor Web Site: http://www.fa-mag.com/news/ria-fined-by-sec-after-hacker-uses-e-mails-to-steal-client-funds-15888.html

[2] *FPPad Home Subscribe What I'm Doing Now Blog About Contact. Why advisers can't trust their clients anymore.*. (2012, April, 11). retrieved December 2015, from FPPad Web Site: http://fppad.com/2012/04/11/why-you-cant-trust-your-clients-anymore/

[3] Markel Cambridge Alliance, *Safeguarding client information and avoiding wire fraud*. (n.d) retrieved January 2016, from Markel Cambridge Alliance Web Site: http://www.markelinsurance.com/risk-management-home/msc-articles/investment-advisors/safeguarding-client-information-and-avioiding-wire-fraud

[4] U.S. Securities and Exchange Commission, (2015, September, 22). *SEC Charges Investment Adviser With Failing to Adopt Proper Cybersecurity Policies and Procedures Prior To Breach*. retrieved December 2015, from SEC Web Site: http://www.sec.gov/news/pressrelease/2015-202.html

[5] Cipriani, J. (2015, June, 15). *Two-factor authentication: What you need to know (FAQ)*. retrieved December 2015, from c|net Web Site: http://www.cnet.com/news/two-factor-authentication-what-you-need-to-know-faq/

[6] Coutin, C. (2015, August, 13). *Educating Clients About Cyber Security Should Be Part of Your Role as an RIA.* retrieved September 13 2015, from Morningstar: ByAllAccounts Web Site: http://byallaccounts.morningstar.com/blog/586-educating-clients-about-cyber-security-should-be-part-of-your-role-as-an-ria.html

Chapter 34 Excess Insurance Fundamentals

[1] Jerry, R. J., & Richmond, D. R. (2012). Excess Insurance. In *Understanding Insurance Law* (5th ed., pp. 975–84). New Providence, NJ: LexisNexis.

[2] Jerry, R. J., & Richmond, D. R. (2012). Defining Insurance. In *Understanding Insurance Law* (5th ed., pp. 10–13). New Providence, NJ: LexisNexis.

[3] Malpractice Insurance Guide 2014. (2014, October). Retrieved August, 2015, from http://cdn.accountingtoday.com/pdfs/ACT1014_Malpractice.pdf

[4] Jerry, R. J., & Richmond, D. R. (2012). Characterizing Insurance Policies. In *Understanding Insurance Law* (5th ed., pp. 975–6). New Providence, NJ: LexisNexis.

[5] Wells, B. (2010, January 4). *Excess Insurance, Umbrella Insurance And Multi-Insurer Coverage Programs* (Rep.). Retrieved January, 2016, from Covington & Burling LLP website: https://www.cov.com/~/media/files/corporate/publications/2010/01/excess-insurance-umbrella-insurance-and-multi-insurer-coverage-programs.pdf

[6] Jerry, R. J., & Richmond, D. R. (2012). Characterizing Insurance Policies. In *Understanding Insurance Law* (5th ed., pp. 976–7). New Providence, NJ: LexisNexis.

[7] http://www.roughnotes.com/rnmagazine/search/commercial_lines/02_08p34.htm

[8] Jerry, R. J., & Richmond, D. R. (2012). Characterizing Insurance Policies. In *Understanding Insurance Law* (5th ed., pp. 975). New Providence, NJ: LexisNexis.

[9] Business Insurance Now, *Business Umbrella Insurance.* (n.d) retrieved April 2016, from Business Insurance Now Web Site: http://www.businessinsurancenow.com/umbrella-liability/

[10] National Association of Insurance Commissioners. (2015, January). *Quarterly Listing of Alien Insurers: Includes Additional Financial and Trust Fund Information* (Rep.). Retrieved December, 2015, from National Association of Insurance Commissioners website: http://www.naic.org/documents/prod_serv_fin_receivership_QLS-AS-206.pdf

[11] American Association of Managing General Agents, *AAMGA FAQ's.* (n.d) retrieved February 2016, from American Association of Managing General Agents Web Site: http://www.aamga.org/faqs

[12] Dearie, J. P., Jr. (Ed.). (2016, January). *Excess and Surplus Lines Laws in the United States: Including Direct Procurement Tax Laws and Industrial Insured Exemptions* (Rep.). Retrieved December, 2015, from Locke Lord LLP website: http://surplusmanual.lockelord.com

[13] American Association of Managing General Agents, *AAMGA FAQ's.* (n.d) retrieved February 2016, from American Association of Managing General Agents Web Site: http://www.aamga.org/faqs

[14] American Association of Managing General Agents, *AAMGA FAQ's.* (n.d) retrieved February 2016, from American Association of Managing General Agents Web Site: http://www.aamga.org/faqs

[15] National Conference of Insurance Guaranty Funds, State Guaranty Fund Web sites. (n.d) retrieved January 2016, from National Conference of Insurance Guaranty Funds Web Site: http://ncigf.org/public-guarantyfundwebsites

[16] Dearie, J. P., Jr. (Ed.). (2016, January). *Excess and Surplus Lines Laws in the United States: Including Direct Procurement Tax Laws and Industrial Insured Exemptions* (Rep.). Retrieved December, 2015, from Locke Lord LLP website: http://surplusmanual.lockelord.com

[17] Jerry, R. J., & Richmond, D. R. (2012). Characterizing Insurance Policies. In *Understanding Insurance Law* (5th ed., pp. 976). New Providence, NJ: LexisNexis.

Chapter 35 Excess Policy Considerations

[1] Will, D., CPA/ABV/CFF, CFE. (2015, November). *Risk Management Best Practices and Current Events*. Lecture presented at CAMICO Policyholder Luncheon, Bethesda, MD.

[2] Johnson, D. (2014, July, 31). *Understanding the Differences Between Standard and Excess/Surplus Lines*. retrieved December 2015, from Claims Journal Web Site: http://www.claimsjournal.com/news/national/2014/07/31/252642.htm

[3] Jerry, R. J., & Richmond, D. R. (2012). Characterizing Insurance Policies. In *Understanding Insurance Law* (5th ed., pp. 976). New Providence, NJ: LexisNexis.

[4] Jerry, R. J., & Richmond, D. R. (2012). Insurers' Liability for Bad Faith. In *Understanding Insurance Law* (5th ed., pp. 162–4). New Providence, NJ: LexisNexis.

[5] Jerry, R. J., & Richmond, D. R. (2012). Insurers' Liability for Bad Faith. In *Understanding Insurance Law* (5th ed., pp. 159–4). New Providence, NJ: LexisNexis.

[6] Shuster, D. J., Esq., & Motley, K. D. (2015, February). The Right to Independent Counsel of Your Choice in the Defense of a Professional Liability Claim. Retrieved February, 2016, from http://www.kramonandgraham.com/siteFiles/News/DJS Article 02-2015.pdf Page 4.

[7] Jerry, R. J., & Richmond, D. R. (2012). Primary & Excess Ins.: Fundamentals & Differences. In *Understanding Insurance Law* (5th ed., pp. 982). New Providence, NJ: LexisNexis.

Chapter 36 Types of Excess Policy Forms

[1] Wells, B. (2010, January 4). *Excess Insurance, Umbrella Insurance And Multi-Insurer Coverage Programs* (Rep.). Retrieved January, 2016, from Covington & Burling LLP website: https://www.cov.com/~/media/files/corporate/publications/2010/01/excess-insurance-umbrella-insurance-and-multi-insurer-coverage-programs.pdf

[2] Malecki, CPCU, D. S. *Risk Management--Umbrella & excess policies-defining terms of coverage*. (n.d) retrieved April 2016, from Rough Notes Web Site: http://www.roughnotes.com/rnmagazine/search/commercial_lines/02_08p34.htm

[3] Wells, B. (2010, January 4). *Excess Insurance, Umbrella Insurance And Multi-Insurer Coverage Programs* (Rep.). Retrieved January, 2016, from Covington & Burling LLP website: https://www.cov.com/~/media/files/corporate/publications/2010/01/excess-insurance-umbrella-insurance-and-multi-insurer-coverage-programs.pdf

[4] Malecki, CPCU, D. S. *Risk Management--Umbrella & excess policies-defining terms of coverage*. (n.d) retrieved April 2016, from Rough Notes Web Site: http://www.roughnotes.com/rnmagazine/search/commercial_lines/02_08p34.htm

[5] Jerry, R. J., & Richmond, D. R. (2012). Characterizing Insurance Policies. In *Understanding Insurance Law* (5th ed., pp. 977). New Providence, NJ: LexisNexis.

[6] Jerry, R. J., & Richmond, D. R. (2012). Characterizing Insurance Policies. In *Understanding Insurance Law* (5th ed., pp. 978). New Providence, NJ: LexisNexis.

Chapter 38 The Pros and Cons of Excess Insurance

[1] Captive.com, The Business to Business Risk & Insurance Exchange, *Excess Insurance*. (n.d) retrieved April 2016, from Captive.com Web Site: http://www.captive.com/art-market/captive-associations/icarfia/excess-insurance

[2] Jerry, R. J., & Richmond, D. R. (2012). Characterizing Insurance Policies. In *Understanding Insurance Law* (5th ed., pp. 976). New Providence, NJ: LexisNexis.

[3] American Association of Managing General Agents, *AAMGA FAQ's*. (n.d) retrieved February 2016, from American Association of Managing General Agents Web Site: http://www.aamga.org/faqs

[4] Malecki, CPCU, D. S. *Risk Management--Umbrella & excess policies-defining terms of coverage.* (n.d) retrieved April 2016, from Rough Notes Web Site: http://www.roughnotes.com/rnmagazine/search/commercial_lines/02_08p34.htm

[5] Jerry, R. J., & Richmond, D. R. (2012). Primary & Excess Ins.: Fundamentals & Differences. In *Understanding Insurance Law* (5th ed., pp. 980). New Providence, NJ: LexisNexis.

[6] Jerry, R. J., & Richmond, D. R. (2012). Primary & Excess Ins.: Fundamentals & Differences. In *Understanding Insurance Law* (5th ed., pp. 981–2). New Providence, NJ: LexisNexis

[7] Dearie, J. P., Jr. (Ed.). (2016, January). *Excess and Surplus Lines Laws in the United States: Including Direct Procurement Tax Laws and Industrial Insured Exemptions* (Rep.). Retrieved December, 2015, from Locke Lord LLP website: http://surplusmanual.lockelord.com

[8] Scislowski, J.D., CPCU, CRIS, R. J. (2010, March). Top 10 Problems with Follow-Form Coverage. retrieved October 2015, from International Risk Management Institute Web Site: http://www.irmi.com/articles/expert-commentary/top-10-problems-with-follow-form-coverage

[9] Ryles, T. (2008, October). Disclosing Policy Limits in Liability Claims: A Landmine for Bad Faith. Retrieved October, 2015, from https://www.irmi.com/articles/expert-commentary/disclosing-policy-limits-in-liability-claims-a-landmine-for-bad-faith

[10] Wilck, D. S., & Shah, K. (2010, November 2). Coverage Concerns In Burning Limits Policies. Retrieved November 18, 2015, from http://www.rivkinradler.com/publications/coverage-concerns-in-burning-limits-policies/

[11] Jerry, R. J., & Richmond, D. R. (2012). Primary & Excess Ins.: Fundamentals & Differences. In *Understanding Insurance Law* (5th ed., pp. 982). New Providence, NJ: LexisNexis

[12] Ryles, T. (2008, October). Disclosing Policy Limits in Liability Claims: A Landmine for Bad Faith. Retrieved October, 2015, from https://www.irmi.com/articles/expert-commentary/disclosing-policy-limits-in-liability-claims-a-landmine-for-bad-faith

[13] Jerry, R. J., & Richmond, D. R. (2012). Characterizing Insurance Policies. In *Understanding Insurance Law* (5th ed., pp. 978). New Providence, NJ: LexisNexis.

[14] Scislowski, J.D., CPCU, CRIS, R. J. (2010, March). Top 10 Problems with Follow-Form Coverage. retrieved October 2015, from International Risk Management Institute Web Site: http://www.irmi.com/articles/expert-commentary/top-10-problems-with-follow-form-coverage

[15] Scislowski, J.D., CPCU, CRIS, R. J. (2010, March). Top 10 Problems with Follow-Form Coverage. retrieved October 2015, from International Risk Management Institute Web Site: http://www.irmi.com/articles/expert-commentary/top-10-problems-with-follow-form-coverage

[16] Jerry, R. J., & Richmond, D. R. (2012). Primary & Excess Ins.: Fundamentals & Differences. In *Understanding Insurance Law* (5th ed., pp. 982–3). New Providence, NJ: LexisNexis

Chapter 39 D&O Insurance Fundamentals

[1] American Institute of Certified Public Accountants, (2007, September). *CPAs As Corporate Directors.* retrieved January 2016, from AICPA Web Site: https://www.cpa2biz.com/Content/media/PRODUCER_CONTENT/Newsletters/Articles_2007/CPA/Sept/Directors.jsp

[2] 107th Congress. (2002, July 30). Public Law 107-204 - Sarbanes-Oxley Act of 2002. Retrieved January, 2016, from https://www.sec.gov/about/laws/soa2002.pdf

[3] American Institute of Certified Public Accountants, (2007, September). *CPAs As Corporate Directors.* retrieved January 2016, from AICPA Web Site: https://www.cpa2biz.com/Content/media/PRODUCER_CONTENT/Newsletters/Articles_2007/CPA/Sept/Directors.jsp

[4] World Law Direct, *Directors' Risks of Personal Liability.* (n.d) retrieved February 2016, from World Law Direct Web Site: http://www.worldlawdirect.com/article/572/directors-risks-personal-liability.html

[5] Chubb Group of Insurance Companies. (n.d.). *Worth the Risk? Highlights from the Chubb 2013 Private Company Risk Survey* (Rep.). Retrieved November, 2016, from Chubb Group of Insurance Companies website: http://www.chubb.com/businesses/csi/chubb12192.pdf

[6] Zurich American Insurance Company. (n.d.). *The Liability Exposures of Nonprofit Board Members: Are the Directors & Officers of Your Organization Protected?* (Rep.). Retrieved February, 2016, from Zurich American Insurance Company website: http://hpd.zurichna.com/Whitepaper/Zurich-Liability-Exposures-Nonprofit.pdf

[7] Towers Watson. (2013). *Directors and Officers Liability Survey: 2012 Summary of Results* (Rep.). Retrieved November, 2015, from Towers Watson website.

[8] Willis Towers Watson. (2004). *D&O FAQ: Directors & Officers (D&O) Liability and Insurance Frequently Asked Questions* (Rep.). Retrieved December, 2015, from Willis Towers Watson website: http://www.willis.com/Documents/Services/Executive Risks/Willis_DandO_FAQ.pdf

[9] Chapman, C. (2015, April, 29). *Advisen Loss Insight: D&O claims trends in Q1 2015*. retrieved February 2016, from Advisen Web Site: http://www.advisenltd.com/2015/04/29/advisen-loss-insight-do-claims-trends-in-q1-2015/

[10] FindLaw, *Directors and Officers Liability Insurance*. (n.d) retrieved April 2016, from FindLaw Web Site: http://corporate.findlaw.com/corporate-governance/directors-and-officers-liability-insurance.html

[11] Willis Towers Watson. (2004). *D&O FAQ: Directors & Officers (D&O) Liability and Insurance Frequently Asked Questions* (Rep.). Retrieved December, 2015, from Willis Towers Watson website: http://www.willis.com/Documents/Services/Executive Risks/Willis_DandO_FAQ.pdf

[12] Willis Towers Watson. (2004). *D&O FAQ: Directors & Officers (D&O) Liability and Insurance Frequently Asked Questions* (Rep.). Retrieved December, 2015, from Willis Towers Watson website: http://www.willis.com/Documents/Services/Executive Risks/Willis_DandO_FAQ.pdf

[13] Zurich American Insurance Company. (n.d.). *The Liability Exposures of Nonprofit Board Members: Are the Directors & Officers of Your Organization Protected?* (Rep.). Retrieved February, 2016, from Zurich American Insurance

Company website: http://hpd.zurichna.com/Whitepaper/Zurich-Liability-Exposures-Nonprofit.pdf

[14] Towers Watson. (2013). *Directors and Officers Liability Survey: 2012 Summary of Results* (Rep.). Retrieved November, 2015, from Towers Watson website.

Chapter 40 Four Basic Components of D&O Coverage

[1] Quillian Yates, Deputy Attorney General, S. (2015, September 9). *Individual Accountability for Corporate Wrongdoing* (Rep.). Retrieved March, 2016, from U.S. Department of Justice: Office of the Deputy Attorney General website: https://www.justice.gov/dag/file/769036/download

[2] Quillian Yates, Deputy Attorney General, S. (2015, September 9). *Individual Accountability for Corporate Wrongdoing* (Rep.). Retrieved March, 2016, from U.S. Department of Justice: Office of the Deputy Attorney General website: https://www.justice.gov/dag/file/769036/download

[3] Resnick, S. & Fuller, J.C. (2016, February, 28). Memo from Justice Department puts corporate directors on notice. retrieved March 2016, from Business Insurance Web Site: http://www.businessinsurance.com/article/20160228/ISSUE0401/302289997/business-insurance-perspectives-stephanie-resnick-john-c-fuller-fox

[4] Dickstein, Shapiro, Morin & Oshinsky. (2005). *A Policyholder's Primer on Insurance* (Rep.). Retrieved February, 2016, from http://www.dicksteinshapiro.com/files/upload/Insurance_Coverage_Primer_A_Policyholder's_Primer_on_Insurance.pdfhttp://www.dicksteinshapiro.com/files/upload/Insurance_Coverage_Primer_A_Policyholder's_Primer_on_Insurance.pdf

[5] Willis Towers Watson. (2004). *D&O FAQ: Directors & Officers (D&O) Liability and Insurance Frequently Asked Questions* (Rep.). Retrieved December, 2015, from Willis Towers Watson website: http://www.willis.com/Documents/Services/Executive Risks/Willis_DandO_FAQ.pdf

[6] Huskins, Esq., P. C. (2014, May, 7). *The ABCs of Your Private Company D&O (Policy Terms)*. retrieved January 2016, from Woodruff Sawyer & Company Web Site: https://wsandco.com/do-notebook/do-abc/

[7] Huskins, Esq., P. C. (2014, May, 7). *The ABCs of Your Private Company D&O (Policy Terms)*. retrieved January 2016, from Woodruff Sawyer & Company Web Site: https://wsandco.com/do-notebook/do-abc/

[8] Dickstein, Shapiro, Morin & Oshinsky. (2005). *A Policyholder's Primer on Insurance* (Rep.). Retrieved February, 2016, from http://www.dicksteinshapiro.com/files/upload/Insurance_Coverage_Primer_A_Policyholder's_Primer_on_Insurance.pdfhttp://www.dicksteinshapiro.com/files/upload/Insurance_Coverage_Primer_A_Policyholder's_Primer_on_Insurance.pdf

[9] FindLaw, *Directors and Officers Liability Insurance*. (n.d) retrieved April 2016, from FindLaw Web Site: http://corporate.findlaw.com/corporate-governance/directors-and-officers-liability-insurance.html

[10] Dickstein, Shapiro, Morin & Oshinsky. (2005). *A Policyholder's Primer on Insurance* (Rep.). Retrieved February, 2016, from http://www.dicksteinshapiro.com/files/upload/Insurance_Coverage_Primer_A_Policyholder's_Primer_on_Insurance.pdfhttp://www.dicksteinshapiro.com/files/upload/Insurance_Coverage_Primer_A_Policyholder's_Primer_on_Insurance.pdf

[11] Towers Watson. (2013). *Directors and Officers Liability Survey: 2012 Summary of Results* (Rep.). Retrieved November, 2015, from Towers Watson website.

[12] Towers Watson. (2013). *Directors and Officers Liability Survey: 2012 Summary of Results* (Rep.). Retrieved November, 2015, from Towers Watson website.

[13] Towers Watson. (2013). *Directors and Officers Liability Survey: 2012 Summary of Results* (Rep.). Retrieved November, 2015, from Towers Watson website.

[14] Allianz Global Corporate & Specialty. (2010). *Introduction to D&O Insurance: Risk Briefing* (Rep.). Retrieved January, 2016, from Allianz Global Corporate & Specialty website: http://www.agcs.allianz.com/assets/PDFs/risk insights/AGCS-DO-infopaper.pdf

[15] Dickstein, Shapiro, Morin & Oshinsky. (2005). *A Policyholder's Primer on Insurance* (Rep.). Retrieved February, 2016, from http://www.dicksteinshapiro.com/files/upload/Insurance_Coverage_Primer_A_Policyholder's_Primer_on_Insurance.pdfhttp://www.dicksteinshapiro.com/files/upload/Insurance_Coverage_Primer_A_Policyholder's_Primer_on_Insurance.pdf

[16] Towers Watson. (2013). *Directors and Officers Liability Survey: 2012 Summary of Results* (Rep.). Retrieved November, 2015, from Towers Watson website.

Chapter 41 Nine Questions to Ask Before Joining a Board

[1] FindLaw, *Directors and Officers Liability Insurance.* (n.d) retrieved April 2016, from FindLaw Web Site: http://corporate.findlaw.com/corporate-governance/directors-and-officers-liability-insurance.html

[2] Melbinger, M.S. (2016, January, 12). *Might Be a Good Time to Review Your Indemnification and D&O Insurance - U.S. Department of Justice to Target Individual Executives (and Their Compensation).* retrieved February 2016, from Lexology Web Site: http://www.lexology.com/library/detail.aspx?g=137f1c17-5af1-4b8f-8405-44cfd27e461c

[3] Towers Watson. (2013). *Directors and Officers Liability Survey: 2012 Summary of Results* (Rep.). Retrieved November, 2015, from Towers Watson website.

[4] LaCroix, K. (2015, July, 15). *Guest Post: D&O What to Know: A Guide to the Evolution of Directors and Officers Insurance from 1933 to the Present.* retrieved March 2016, from The D&O Diary: A Periodic Journal Containing Items of Interest From the World of Directors & Officers Liability, With Occasional Commentary Web Site: http://www.dandodiary.com/2016/02/articles/d-o-insurance/guest-post-do-what-to-know-a-guide-to-the-evolution-of-directors-and-officers-insurance-from-1933-to-the-present/

[5] Quillian Yates, Deputy Attorney General, S. (2015, September 9). *Individual Accountability for Corporate Wrongdoing* (Rep.). Retrieved March, 2016, from U.S. Department of Justice: Office of the Deputy Attorney General website: https://www.justice.gov/dag/file/769036/download

66 AON Corporation. (2010). *Http://www.aon.com/attachments/thought-leadership/Peer_Benchmarking_DO_Executive_Summary_08112010.pdf* (Rep.). Retrieved January, 2016, from NASDAQ OMX website: http://www.aon.com/attachments/thought-leadership/Peer_Benchmarking_DO_Executive_Summary_08112010.pdf

7 Wayne, A. E. (n.d.). Questions Concerning D&O Coverage [Telephone interview].

After graduating from DePaul University in 1991, Alex worked for Internet Intermediaries, a national reinsurance broker. Alex has obtained an Associate in Reinsurance (ARe), Chartered Property Casualty Underwriter (CPCU), Associate in Surplus Lines Insurance (ASLI) and Registered Professional Liability Underwriter (RPLU). He built a book of professional liability to over $35M and manages a staff of nine brokers and six support staff. Alex served as the Chairperson and is a long standing board member of the Association of Lloyd's Brokers. He is also a frequent presenter on professional liability at conferences.

8 Willis Towers Watson. (2004). *D&O FAQ: Directors & Officers (D&O) Liability and Insurance Frequently Asked Questions* (Rep.). Retrieved December, 2015, from Willis Towers Watson website: http://www.willis.com/Documents/Services/Executive Risks/Willis_DandO_FAQ.pdf

9 United States Department of Labor, *Meeting Your Fiduciary Responsibilities*. (n.d) retrieved April 2016, from United States Department of Labor Web Site: http://www.dol.gov/ebsa/publications/fiduciaryresponsibility.html

10 FindLaw, *Directors and Officers Liability Insurance*. (n.d) retrieved April 2016, from FindLaw Web Site: http://corporate.findlaw.com/corporate-governance/directors-and-officers-liability-insurance.html

11 Huskins, Esq., P. C. (2014, May, 7). *The ABCs of Your Private Company D&O (Policy Terms)*. retrieved January 2016, from Woodruff Sawyer & Company Web Site: https://wsandco.com/do-notebook/do-abc/

[12] Dickstein, Shapiro, Morin & Oshinsky. (2005). *A Policyholder's Primer on Insurance* (Rep.). Retrieved February, 2016, from http://www.dicksteinshapiro.com/files/upload/Insurance_Coverage_Primer_A_Policyholder's_Primer_on_Insurance.pdfhttp://www.dicksteinshapiro.com/files/upload/Insurance_Coverage_Primer_A_Policyholder's_Primer_on_Insurance.pdf

[13] Dickstein, Shapiro, Morin & Oshinsky. (2005). *A Policyholder's Primer on Insurance* (Rep.). Retrieved February, 2016, from http://www.dicksteinshapiro.com/files/upload/Insurance_Coverage_Primer_A_Policyholder's_Primer_on_Insurance.pdfhttp://www.dicksteinshapiro.com/files/upload/Insurance_Coverage_Primer_A_Policyholder's_Primer_on_Insurance.pdf

[14] Huskins, Esq., P. C. (2014, May, 7). *The ABCs of Your Private Company D&O (Policy Terms)*. retrieved January 2016, from Woodruff Sawyer & Company Web Site: https://wsandco.com/do-notebook/do-abc/

[15] Ace Group. (2005, July). D&O Policy Terms: Know What to Ask For. *Ace Media Centre*. Retrieved March, 2016, from http://www.ace-group.com/bm-en/media-centre/do-policy-terms-know-what-to-ask-for.aspx

[16] Wayne, A. E. (n.d.). Questions Concerning D&O Coverage [Telephone interview].

[17] FindLaw, *Directors and Officers Liability Insurance*. (n.d) retrieved April 2016, from FindLaw Web Site: http://corporate.findlaw.com/corporate-governance/directors-and-officers-liability-insurance.html

Chapter 42 Executive Summary

[1] Company, A. M. (2014). Important Functions of Insurance Organizations. In *Understanding the Insurance Industry: An Overview for Those Working With and in One of the World's Most Interesting and Vital Industries* (2014 ed., pp. 11–12). AM Best Company.

Fair Winds & Following Seas.

Made in the USA
Middletown, DE
07 June 2016